# Fourth G[illegible]
# Language

## Reading Book 3
Lessons 101 to 160

Visit **McRuffy.com** for helpful resources to teach this curriculum!


**Reading Book 3**
ISBN 9781592692422

**McRuffy Press Fourth Grade Language Arts Curriculum**
978159269-1555



Written and illustrated by
Brian Davis M. A. Ed.

Graphic Design by
Sherylynn Davis

McRuffy Press, LLC
P.O. Box 212
Raymore, MO 64083

816-331-7831

sales@mcruffy.com

**www.McRuffy.com**

## Book 3 Table of Contents

# Noggin

Story and illustrations by
Brian Davis



## Vocabulary Words

apatosaurus
brontosaurus
demonstrated
Europe
extinguisher
farsighted
gibberish
glacier
interpreter
irresistible
mammoth
mysterious
plesiosaur
prehistoric
pterodactyl
translated
transportation
Ukraine

Have you ever sat around a campfire and heard a story? Grab a s'more and listen in as a dad tells a story to his family about a cave girl named Noggin and her amazing discoveries and adventures with incredible animals.

# Chapter 1
## The Campfire

Will you tell us a story, Dad?" asked Mary, the youngest, as she pulled the marshmallow out of the fire and puffed until the flame was out.

"Has everyone had enough s'mores?" asked her mom. "You know once he gets started there's no turning back."

"What does that mean?" asked her dad as he placed another log on the campfire.

"Your stories can go on and on," said the mom. She saw the look on her husband's face. "And they're so entertaining that we wouldn't want to be distracted by eating."

"Nice save," said Dad.

"Tell us a story about a prince and a princess," said Ashley. "Make it really romantic."

"Romantic?" protested Michael, the oldest of the three children. "Make it interesting, like a story about racing cars."

"How can that be interesting?" asked Ashley. "They just drive around in circles for hours. What kind of story is that? The cars took a lap and another lap and another lap. Why not just tell a story about a golf game?"

"Can it be miniature golf?" asked Mary. "I like playing miniature golf."

"I wasn't serious," frowned Ashley as she bit into a chocolaty, gooey s'more. That took her frown away very quickly.

"I've got a story," said Dad as he watched the flames dance among the logs. "It's perfect for a campout because it's about the discovery of fire. It all began a long time ago…"

"That's not right," said Mary.

"I haven't even told anything about the story yet," said Dad.

"It's supposed to start with: Once upon a time."

"Okay," sighed Dad. "Once upon a time…"

"See, that's much better," said Mary. "I like it already."

Dad nodded and continued, "there was an ice age and big glaciers started covering the land."

"I thought you said this was about fire, not ice," commented Michael.

"I'll get to it," answered Dad. "Give me some time."

"Lots of time," teased Mom.

"A tribe of cavemen and women were trying to outrun a glacier," continued Dad.

"Uh…Dad, glaciers move really slow, like a few miles a year. I don't think it would be too hard to outrun them," said Ashley

Dad scrunched his eyebrows and gave her *that* look.

"Okay," sighed Ashley. "But this better have some romance in it."

"As I was saying," continued Dad. "The cavemen were fleeing the glacier. They were riding giant far-sighted turtles."

"Giant far-sighted turtles?" giggled Mary.

"That's why they were having difficulty outrunning the glaciers. The turtles saw a giant boulder and thought it was another turtle. They fell deeply in love with the boulder.

They called it Shelly. So great was their love that they risked their lives to try to push it out of the way of the glacier that was speeding toward them," said Dad.

"Did you say the turtles fell in love with a boulder?" asked Mom.

"Ashley wanted romance in the story," said Dad.

"Hopelessly romantic," joked Michael as he pretended to hug himself. "But why would they ride something slow like a turtle?"

"They couldn't catch the giant snails," answered Dad.

"Are you sure you don't want to tell a story about racing cars?" asked Michael. "I think the story would move a lot faster."

"Don't count on it," said his mom.

"Not if I keep getting interrupted," agreed Dad. "Now where was I?"

"Turtles were kissing rocks," said Mary, "because they were in love."

"So," continued Dad, "the cavemen needed to move the rock. They decided to have a meeting to discuss how to move the rock. Now the name of the caveman tribe was the Bugmi tribe."

"They were once a part of a bigger tribe of cavemen. But the cave people in the Bugmi tribe were not the brightest of the bunch. Often times the other cavemen would point to them and say, you bug me! That's how they got their name. One day, all the other cavemen snuck away and left the Bugmi tribe all alone."

"I know just how they felt," said Mary. "Michael and Ashley did the same thing to me this afternoon. They told me we were playing hide and seek and to count to a million when it was my turn. It's a good thing I know how to count by ten thousands or I would still be counting."

"The Bugmies could have used someone like you," said Dad. "They were playing pin the tail on the wooly mammoth. The cavemen gave the Bugmies mammoth tails and blindfolded them. They were then spun around in circles. After that, all the other cavemen rode away on the backs of giant prehistoric squirrels. They were tired of the Bugmies."

“A caveman named Oof was the first to remove his blindfold. Yet, it was too late. The other cavemen were gone. Oof then pulled the blindfolds off the other Bugmies. They were so grateful that he restored their sight that they chose him to be their new chief.”

“He was soon married to a beautiful cavegirl named Arp. Soon they had a baby boy. They couldn’t decide on a name, so they let the baby name himself. When he was born he began to cry. So they called him Wah! Wah! Wah! His nickname was Wah.”

“Next, they had a girl. When she was born she started crying, Wah! So they named her Already Says Her Brother’s Name. She definitely needed a nickname, so they called her Ash.”

“Hey, isn’t that a bit close to my name?” asked Ashley.

“If it is, then that makes me Wah!” protested Michael.

“Who am I? I’m born next,” said Mary.

“Oof and Arp did have one more child,” their dad continued with the story. “They decided that having the babies name themselves was not working out so well.”

“Oof grunted to Arp, ‘Must find name for baby girl.’”

“Arp pointed to Oof’s head and suggested, ‘Use noggin.’”

“Oof said, ‘Good idea. We call her Noggin.’”

## Chapter 2
## They Call It Turtle Love

"Wait, the Bugmies were being chased by a glacier and then all the other cavemen left them behind and Oof and his wife had three children," commented Ashley

"No," said Dad. "The cavemen left the Bugmies before the glacier came. The children were born after the other cavemen left and before the glacier came."

"That's not what you said," replied Ashley.

"I started telling the story, and then decided to give a little background information," explained Dad. "So you'd understand better."

"But now I understand less," said Ashley.

"I understand," said Mary. "The turtles fell in love, Oof fell in love, and I was born and called Noggin."

"It's not a story about us," said Michael. "Dad's just making it up."

"Although, sometimes Mary does bug me," said Ashley.

"If you want to hear the end of the story before sunrise, you better let your father talk," said Mom.

"Thanks, Dear," said Dad. "Now, back to the glacier. The Bugmies needed to move the boulder named Shelly to make the turtles move. Oof was getting desperate. The glacier was moving in. If he didn't come up with a solution in the next few months, the Bugmies would almost certainly be crushed."

"Why didn't they just run away?" asked Michael. "It would be a lot quicker."

"I'll get to that later," said Dad.

"The Bugmies can't run away!" cried Mary. "The glacier will run over the turtles."

"Don't worry," said Dad. "Giant turtles were the sports car of the caveman age. They still had several payments to make on them. The Bugmies couldn't just leave them behind."

"Didn't they get the glacier insurance for the turtles?" asked Ashley.

"Nobody said the Bugmies were too bright," explained Dad, "Which was a real problem when they needed a solution and needed it fast. Besides, the next best choice was to strap giant beetles to their knees. Sometimes it worked. Sometimes it just got squishy."

"I thought they had a few months to find a solution," said Michael.

"I said they weren't too bright," said Dad. "One day Oof climbed to the top of the boulder hoping to be inspired with an idea for moving it. All the other Bugmies gathered around the rock, squeezing in between the lovesick turtles.

As Oof walked around his foot slipped on some gravel. A rock the size of a baseball bounded down the side of the giant boulder. It hit Noggin right on her noggin."

"Ouch!" cried Mary. "Wouldn't that hurt me?"

"Noggin was smart," said Dad. "Much smarter than the average Bugmi. She wore a tortoise shell helmet. The rock bounced right off her head and hit Wah on the hand. He started shaking it and crying out, while dancing around."

Dad demonstrated Wah's movement. He looked like he was strumming an air guitar.

"Oof looked over the edge and yelled, 'What make loud sound?'"

"Noggin answered, 'Rock roll!'"

"Oof nodded happily and said, 'Oof like rock roll music. Catchy tune. Like lyrics, Wah! Wah! Wah!' Oof sang along."

"Noggin tried to correct her father. She explained, 'Rock roll, hit Wah.'"

"Oof nodded happily, 'Wah good, but not sure song will be a rock roll hit. Too bad radio not invented yet. Maybe he should write turtle love song. Might help.'"

"Dad!" said Ashley. "Are you saying that was the invention of rock and roll music?"

"Like Oof said," answered Dad. "It didn't really catch on until the radio was invented."

"The important thing," Dad continued, "Is that the rock bouncing off Noggin's noggin gave her an idea."

"She smiled and said, 'We roll boulder. Turtles will follow. Leave glacier in the dust!'"

"Oof smiled, 'That my girl! We do as she say. We roll boulder. Wah sing rock roll song, inspire us."

"Hey, what about Ash? Didn't she do anything," asked Ashley.

"It's funny you should ask" said Dad. "Already Says Her Brother's Name, or Ash as she was called, stood around and asked a lot of questions and talked about how romantic it was that the turtles loved the boulder."

"That's not very realistic," complained Ashley.

Everybody looked at Ashley, smiled, and nodded.

"You guys think you are so clever. How are the Bugmies going to make the rock roll?" Ashley asked.

"You ask so many questions, Ashley," teased Michael.

"But that is a good question," added her mother.

Dad thought for a few seconds, "Okay, all the Bugmies cheered Noggin's idea. Then Ash spoke up. 'How we make boulder roll? It very heavy.'"

“Oof answered, ‘Ash always asks many questions but good questions. I have idea. I hit Noggin with bigger rock and she get bigger idea!”

“Noggin shook her head, ‘No! No! I have idea. No need to hit Noggin with rock.’”

“You sure?” asked Oof. “Have nice big rock right here, size of basketball, whatever that is.”

“Noggin sure, no need to hit with rock,” said Noggin. “We slide rock to hill, then rock will roll.”

“How we make rock slide?” asked Ash.

“Put rock on something slippery,” suggested Noggin.

“But me don’t know rock slide music,” cried Wah.

“Where we get slippery stuff?” asked Ash.

“Need to be slippery, like ice,” said Oof.

Mom spoke up, “Where was the mom this whole time? What ever happened to Arp?”

“Oops,” said Dad. “I didn’t mean to leave anyone out. Let me see…I got it. Arp said, ‘Need to be slippery like ice.’”

“Where we get ice?” asked Oof.

“How about huge glacier behind us?” suggested Noggin.

“Oof asked, ‘How you get such great ideas?’ You smart like your mom. Me never thought of huge wall of glacier rushing toward us.’”

Dad looked at Mom and winked.

“It’s so nice to be included,” said Mom.

“No problem,” smiled Dad. “So Arp said, ‘Get glacier ice. Let’s move this boulder along. Have mammoth meatloaf in oven. Want to eat dinner before sunrise.”

“Wait a minute,” said Michael. “You said this was a story about the discovery of fire. How could they cook in an oven if they didn’t have fire?”

“Don’t be silly,” said Mary. “Microwave ovens don’t use fire to cook.”

“Me silly?” protested Michael. “They didn’t have microwave ovens or the electricity to run them.”

“Oh,” said Mary. “Then what did they do?”

“They waited a long time before dinner was ready,” said Dad. “Then they ordered carryout.”

## Chapter 3
## Shelly

"I think this story is missing something," said Mom.

"What's that?" asked Dad.

"I was thinking a plot," suggested Mom.

Dad sighed in relief, "I thought you were going to say an ending."

"I know what it's missing," said Mary. "It's missing a bad guy."

"How about some romance not involving rocks and turtles," suggested Ashley.

"I think a monster would be a good idea. How about a monster driving a sports car?" suggested Michael.

"They didn't have sports cars back then," argued Ashley.

"I know," said Michael. "Maybe the sports car could even be a time machine."

"I think I saw those movies," said Dad. "Let me continue with the story. The Bugmies slid the boulder on sheets of glacial ice to the edge of a hill. They used turtle power to push it. Next, the boulder rolled down a hill. The turtles raced behind it."

"How could the turtles move that fast?" asked Ashley.

"Noggin was smart enough and thoughtful enough to tie ice to their feet too. They slid right down the hill. The boulder slammed into a wall of rock in the valley below."

"The whole Bugmi tribe slid down the ice after the turtles. Wah was the first to notice the crack in the boulder. The ice skating turtles noticed the crack too. They suddenly zipped on down the valley."

"So they weren't in love with the boulder anymore?" asked Mary.

"No," Dad sighed dramatically. "The giant ice skating turtles got cold feet."

Mom rolled her eyes, "Don't tell me. They got cold feet because they were covered with ice."

Dad smiled, "It was just as well because the boulder wasn't really a boulder. The turtles were right to call it Shelly. It turns out the boulder was a shell and whatever was in it was beginning to hatch."

"Oof moved in for a closer look. Suddenly, a tongue shot out of the crack. It licked the chief and lifted him right off the ground. The caveman landed right on his rump. When he looked back up, he was staring right into the nostrils of a baby brontosaurus."

"Uh Dad," interrupted Michael. "It's called an Apatosaurus, now."

"When did it change?" asked Dad.

"I think the early 1900's. Maybe it hadn't changed when you were in school," Michael joked.

"So is this story taking place before or after the 1900's?" Dad asked Michael.

"It does have cavemen in it. I'd say that was before the 1900's," said Michael.

"Then brontosaurus it is," said Dad. "The cavemen weren't very up to date on dinosaur names. Most of the dinosaurs were already extinct. In fact this was the first real brontosaurus Oof had ever seen. Sure, he had read about them on the history walls in his elementary school cave, but the brontosaurus was much more lifelike in real life."

"They had school in a cave?" asked Mary.

"That would be cool," said Michael.

"About 52 degrees year around," said Dad.

"I meant it would be really fun," said Michael.

"He knew what you meant," said Mom. "He's just giving you a difficult time."

"But not as difficult of a time as the Bugmies were going through," said Dad. "Now that the turtles were gone, they were without transportation. There was nothing to do but sit around the valley and wait. All the time the glacier was racing toward them. If it reached the valley before they left, they could be buried in ice. That would be very cool too, but not really fun."

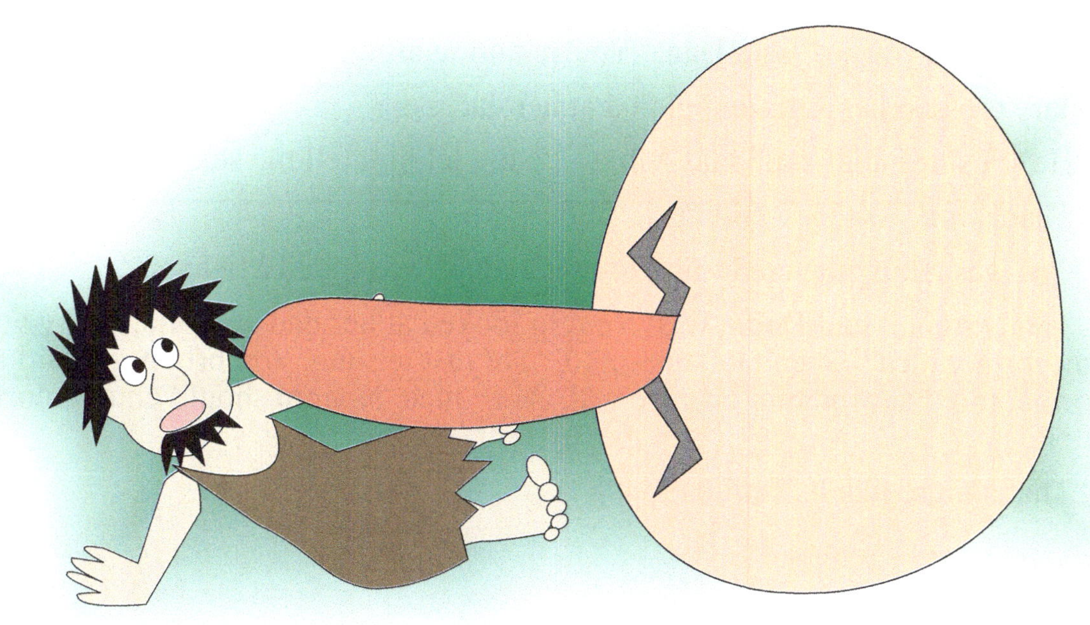

"The Bugmies had no plan. They were very afraid. That is all but one Bugmi. Noggin was busy everyday. She picked fruit, vegetables, and grass. Noggin didn't eat it. She fed it to Shelly the brontosaurus. Although Shelly started out big, the dinosaur grew bigger and bigger."

"One day Noggin climbed onto the back of Shelly. She sat on the head of the brontosaurus. 'Up Shelly,' commanded Noggin. The dinosaur lifted her up into the air. When she reached the top of the valley, she could see the glacier. It was about to tumble down onto the Bugmi tribe."

"Noggin commanded Shelly to duck back down. Next, she let out a whistle to get the attention of the tribe. Noggin warned them about the closeness of the glacier. Oof was very worried. 'We need plan. If only we had giant turtles back. Now we have nothing to ride out of here.'"

"Climb up on Shelly's back," Noggin told them.

"That good idea," said Oof. "Always think more clearly on dinosaur back. Maybe even see turtles we can ride."

"Noggin wrapped a vine around Shelly's long neck. She told the all the Bugmies to hold onto the vine. Then Noggin spoke to Shelly the brontosaurus. 'Go Shelly.'"

"The dinosaur walked forward. All the Bugmies were surprised. Now brontosauruses weren't exactly as fast as cheetahs, but they were much, much faster than the giant turtles. To the Bugmies the brontosaurus seemed as fast as lightning."

"Newfangled dinosaur very fast!" yelled Oof as he gripped the vine as tightly as he could. "Hey, I got idea. We ride brontosaurus out of valley. Much better than slow poke giant turtles. Good thing Bugmies have brilliant chief like me."

"Wait," protested Mary. "Noggin was the one that thought of riding Shelly. Why is Oof taking all the credit?"

"Now, Mary, next thing you know you'll want to take the credit for the coloring contest I won last year," said Dad.

"I won the coloring contest!" corrected Mary.

"See, I told you so," said Dad. "You're taking all the credit."

Mary crossed her arms and glared at her dad.

"He's just teasing you," said Ashley. "Now let him tell the story."

"Thank you, Ashley," said Dad. "Where was I?"

"Oof was taking the credit for Noggin's idea," reminded Michael.

"That's right," said Dad. "Well Noggin looked at her dad and said, 'Why you take credit for my idea?' Then Oof answered, 'Me just teasing. You bright girl and good at coloring, too. I saw picture on cave wall. Very nice. Noggin should enter coloring contest."

"That's more like it," smiled Mary.

## Chapter 4
## Bugmi Feet

"A brontosaurus is very long. About 15 feet long when they're fully grown," said Dad.

"Actually, an Apatosaurus could grow up to 90 feet long and weigh 30 tons," corrected Michael.

"Not if they're hit with a shrink laser beam mounted to a hood of a race car that was also a time machine," said Dad.

"Is that what happened?" asked Ashley. "And if it did, how would all the Bugmies be able to ride it?"

"Maybe they got hit by the shrink laser beam too," suggested Mary. "Is that what happened, Dad?"

"No," said Dad. "That was my mistake. I meant to say 15 meters."

Michael pulled out his calculator. He punched in the numbers. "Still doesn't work. You're about 45 feet short."

"I was measuring with a Bugmi ruler. They're about 6 feet long compared to our rulers."

Michael punched more numbers into the calculator and sighed, "Okay, 15 Bugmi feet equal 90 of our feet."

"Did the Bugmies really have feet that were 6 feet long?" asked Mary.

"No," said Dad. "Their feet were about the same size as ours. Six Bugmies were chosen to decide how long a foot should be. They couldn't decide whose foot to use, so they used all their right feet. The bad part was, every time they wanted to measure something, those same six Bugmies had to line up their feet. And each time they washed their feet they had to redraw their inch lines."

"That's a terrible way to measure," said Ashley.

"It was worse when they had to decide how heavy was a pound," added Dad. "According to Bugmi measurements, Shelly only weighed 5 pounds. It took the whole tribe just to measure an ounce."

"This isn't really moving the story along," said Mom.

"I know," said Dad. "I was just giving Shelly and the Bugmies time to get out of the valley."

Mom frowned.

"Okay," said Dad. "I think they're about out now, but not quite. The only way out of the valley was a tunnel. As we all know, brontosauruses are afraid of tunnels."

"How would we know that?" asked Michael. "I don't think it's an established fact that an Apatosaurus would be afraid of a tunnel."

"How would anyone know that?" agreed Ashley.

"Next thing you're going to tell me is that you didn't know brontosauruses were afraid of bunny rabbits."

"I didn't know that," said Mary. "But it makes sense to me."

"Why?" laughed Mom.

"Because a brontosaurus tail is shaped like a giant carrot," explained Mary. "Maybe that's why they went extinct. Bunnies kept biting their tails."

Dad smiled, "Have you heard this story before?"

"No," said Mary. "I'm just smart like Noggin."

"And Noggin was very smart," agreed Dad. "She realized right away that Shelly wouldn't go into the tunnel. The Bugmies became more frightened when they heard a loud crash behind them. It was debris being pushed by the glacier. It was closing in on them fast."

"Noggin saw a bush filled with large red berries. She slid down off the brontosaurus. Next, she filled a turtle shell with the berries and mashed them into a thick paste. Noggin used the red paste to draw a bunny on a rock next to the tunnel. Shelly began to get very concerned. Then Noggin drew a circle around the picture and a slash through it."

"No bunnies allowed," said Mary.

"That's right," said Dad. "Now, Shelly was still afraid of the tunnel. The Bugmies were still afraid of getting crushed by the glacier. So Noggin put in place the rest of her plan. She snuck behind Shelly and started singing like a bunny."

"Dad," corrected Michael, "rabbits don't sing."

"Prehistoric bunnies could sing. Unfortunately, none of their recordings have survived," said Dad. "They weren't the best musicians, but they could sing quite well."

"I don't believe you," said Ashley.

"I do," said Mary. "I once saw a movie about singing chipmunks, so I'm sure rabbits could sing at one time too."

Mom looked at her watch, "I think you should just let him tell the story Ashley."

“Thank you,” said Dad. “The Bugmies were thankful, too. When Noggin sang her bunny song, Shelly started into the tunnel. All the Bugmies cheered. Noggin jumped onto Shelly’s tail. Noggin let out a huge sigh of relief.”

“Then just as the entrance of the tunnel was fading from view, she caught a glimpse of furry creatures staring at a rock. It was a group of bunnies singing a sad song. Their only hope of escape from the glacier was blocked by a no bunny sign. It was a matter of time before they would be crushed by the glacier.”

“Oh no!” cried Mary. “Is that how singing bunnies became extinct?”

“Noggin couldn’t let that happen,” said Dad. “She climbed to the end of Shelly’s tail and hopped off. The tail was so long that Noggin tumbled right to the feet of the bunnies. She tried to nudge the bunnies into the tunnel, but they kept pointing at the no bunny sign and frowning. Finally, Noggin noticed the turtle shell she left at the base of the rock.”

“Thinking quickly, she painted an arrow away from the entrance of the tunnel. Now it looked the rabbits weren’t allowed to stay *out of* the tunnel. The bunnies smiled. Now they had no choice but to find safety from the glacier in the tunnel. Noggin got them to promise not to bite Shelly’s tail and to not sing and frighten the brontosaur. The bunnies all agreed.”

“I see,” said Mary. “And the bunnies thought they were promising to never sing again. Noggin only meant while they were in the tunnel.”

“Exactly right,” said Dad. “Prehistoric bunnies took promises very seriously. Because of this simple misunderstanding, they never sang again. After generations and generations of bunnies, they even forgot they could sing.”

“That’s so sad. If only we could teach them,” sighed Mary. “I would love to hear singing bunnies. Can we get a bunny and sign it up for singing lessons?”

Mom laughed, “I don’t think it would work that way.”

“So Michael and Ashley, there you have it,” said Dad. “That’s the reason no one alive has ever heard a bunny sing. Now do you still think I’m making all of this up?”

“Yes!” the both answered at the same time.

## Chapter 5
## Wok, Wok

Mom put another log on the fire.

"Now that was a nice story,"' she smiled. "Maybe we should call it a night and get some rest."

"Rest!" said Dad. "We can stay here and get rest, the rest of the story that is!"

"Yes!" agreed Mary.

"There's more?" asked Mom. She looked at her watch. Then she unhooked the band and put it in her pocket. "We are on vacation. Why do I need to worry about the time?"

"You don't need to worry about the time," said Dad, "But Noggin had a time problem. She was out of it. The glacier rumbled into the valley. It caused the ground to quake. That made rocks tumble and block the entrance to the tunnel. Noggin was separated from her family for the first time in her life."

"That wasn't her worst problem. More of the glacier was tumbling into the valley. She climbed up the rocks in front of the tunnel. She hoped to find even a small opening that she could squeeze through. But it was not to be."

"The glacier was closing in too fast. Noggin grabbed a vine and started pulling herself up the side of the cliff. Higher and higher she climbed until she reached the top. Noggin stood on the other side of the valley. She could see the glacier filling it up. It was only a matter of days before the glacier could continue moving on her side."

"She thought she saw a path that could lead to the other side of the mountain. The other Bugmies had to be on the other side by now. There was one huge problem. Noggin couldn't find anything to ride, not even a beetle. She was alone and afraid. She looked down at the ground and cried."

"Tears dropped on her toes. That made them wiggle. Noggin noticed the movement and began to explore the mysterious wiggling, tear stained creatures on the ground. She knelt down to get a closer look and noticed something else strange. The wiggling creatures were attached to her leg. There was even a flat part between her leg and the creatures."

"Wait!" said Ashley. "Are you telling me that Noggin was discovering her feet for the first time ever?"

"She was the discoverer of feet," said Dad.

"Wow!" said Mary. "Look, I have feet too!"

"Seriously?" asked Michael. "Are you just now figuring that out?"

"I'm just teasing," laughed Mary.

Mom smiled, "I remember the day you discovered your feet, Michael. You were just a baby. You could fit three toes in your mouth."

"Oh, Michael," said Mary, "Show us!"

"Yuck," said Ashley.

"Noggin discovered more than her feet that day," said Dad. "As she thought about her feet, she wondered what they were used for. She stood up again because her father Oof had taught her that the best thinking places are higher up. The problem was, now she couldn't see her feet as well."

"She moved her right leg forward. That was better. She could see one foot. Now, she wanted to see the other. She moved her left leg forward. Noggin could see her left foot, but she moved the leg too far. She could no longer see the right foot."

"We get the picture, Dad," said Ashley. "She was walking."

"Yes," said Dad, "But do you know how walking got its name?"

"No," answered Ashley.

"Well," said Dad. "As you know, prehistoric grass made sounds when it was stepped on. The grass Noggin was standing on made a 'wok' sound when it was stepped on. So as Noggin moved along, she heard the sound."

"Me wok, wok," said Noggin.

"She later shortened it to wok," continued Dad.

"Noggin was so smart," said Mary.

"It's really a good thing Noggin was standing on the wok grass. If she made her discovery on the other patch of grass to her right, she would have named it urkelgook. Could you imagine? Instead of walking, we would be urkelgooking," said Dad.

"And a sideurkelgook would be in front of our house," Mary added.

"That just sounds messy," said Mom.

"Wait, how do we know prehistoric grass made sounds?" asked Michael.

"Uh, Michael," said Mom. "Remember the whole singing bunny discussion? Do you really want to go through that again?"

"Why don't you just continue with the story, Dad?" Michael quickly suggested.

"No problem," said Dad. "Well, the discovery of walking led to the discovery of a great walking accessory. As Noggin walked toward the path up the mountain, she found something blocking her path. A branch had fallen off a tree. It was in her way."

"Noggin bent down to the limb and said, 'Walk stick. Get out of way.'"

"Noggin stared at the stick and finally spoke to it again, 'Stick no walk? I teach walk stick. Noggin good at walk."

“She picked it up and starting walking with it. She named it Stick. That’s how the walking stick was invented,” concluded Dad.

“I wish I had an urkelgookingstick,” said Mary. “That would be fun.”

“More than that,” said Dad. “The walking stick was an important step to the development of Noggin’s greatest discovery. Sure, she taught the stick to walk, but in turn, the stick would teach her something very important.”

“Wait,” said Michael, “Are you telling me prehistoric sticks could talk?”

“Of course not!” exclaimed Dad. “That would just be silly. You know I don’t tell silly stories.”

“Never,” agreed Mom, but her expression and tone of voice said the opposite.

“Exactly,” said Dad. “Noggin continued up the path. Before long she came to a strange sight. There was a path of rectangular rocks that led up to the top of the mountain. Each stone was offset from the other. Noggin climbed and climbed. She was glad the walking stick was with her. They were becoming best friends and helped each other walk up the steep trail.”

“I’ve heard of dogs being man’s best friend, but sticks? I’ve never heard of that,” said Michael.

“Dogs being man’s best friend came much later,” Dad explained. “That all started when someone lost their pet stick and a dog retrieved it. That made the man so grateful; the dog became one of his best friends too.

## Chapter 6
## A Ferocious Peep

"So did Noggin find her family?" asked Mary. "I wouldn't want her to be lost forever. I can't imagine how afraid she must have been."

"I'll get to that," said Dad. "Noggin climbed up the mysterious rocks."

"You've already told us that," said Michael.

"But I didn't tell you what she saw at the top," said Dad.

"What?" asked Mary.

"More rocks," smiled Dad.

"I think the story is getting a little boring," commented Ashley. "There really needs to be something more exciting than rocks."

"Well, Noggin saw a strange looking rock. It was long and thin. The most mysterious thing about it was that it was hooked to another rock," said Dad in a hushed, mysterious tone of voice.

"The way you're telling it is not boring," said Ashley. "It's all this talk about rocks. I mean what else would you expect on a mountain?"

"Okay," said Dad. "Suddenly a big, furry creature popped out from behind a rock. It let out a ferocious peep."

"Peeps aren't ferocious," said Mary. "They're yummy."

"Not the candy," corrected Dad. "The sound."

"Mary's right," said Michael. "A peep does not sound ferocious."

"It does when it comes from a giant peeping bearasaurus!" said Dad.

"There's no such thing as a bearasaurus," said Michael. "And if there were it would make more of a growling sound."

"Then what do you call the large, peeping, bear-like animal that was growling at Noggin?" asked Dad.

"Maybe it was an Arctodus simus," suggested Michael. "That was a giant bear that is now extinct. Although I highly doubt they peeped. It just doesn't seem consistent with bear-like qualities. They would have stood about twelve feet tall."

"That's about two feet tall in Bugmi measurements," said Mary.

"I think the bearasaurus is a figment of your dad's imagination." offered Mom. "But is there any point in arguing this?"

"That's why it was peeping," said Dad.

"I don't understand," said Ashley.

"The point!" smiled Dad. "The point of a thorn was sticking in the paw of the bearasaurus. Everyone knows that when a bearasaurus gets a splinter or a thorn in its paw it starts peeping."

"Why would it do that?" asked Mary.

"Nobody would want to help a growling, snarling bearasaurus. They wouldn't even want to come close to one. A peeping bearasaurus is so cute that it is irresistible. Noggin just had to help out the bearasaurus. But there was one problem. Advanced techniques in thorn pulling had not been invented yet."

"I should have known it," Michael shook his head.

"Normally, they climbed a tree. Then they tied a rope around the thorn and tied the other end to a branch. Then all they had to do was jump out of the tree."

"How could you tie a rope around a thorn?" asked Michael.

"Thorns were much bigger back then," explained Dad. "Noggin had a problem. There were no trees on the top of the mountain. She sat down on a rock. Noggin expected to think of a solution very quickly. She was, after all, high up on a mountain. Noggin sat and took a deep breath."

"That's when she noticed a strange smell. It was coming from just a little higher up the path. There was also something very strange in the air. It was like a cloud, but smellier."

"I think it was smoke!" said Mary. "Is Noggin finally going to get to discover fire?"

"Noggin and the walking stick decided to climb a little higher. They told the bearasaurus to wait right where he was and they would be right back," said Dad. "Noggin was about to make a big discovery. Yet, she never took all the credit. Noggin couldn't have done it without her walking stick."

"As she reached the top of the path, Noggin saw something glowing," said Dad. "She had never seen such a strange sight. It was at that moment that the walking stick decided to get a little closer look."

"Sticks don't have eyes," said Mary. "How could it look?"

"Fortunately, Noggin carried a potato with her. As you know, potatoes have eyes."

"But they can't see!" objected Ashley.

"The potatoes that grew on the potato trees could see," said Dad. "It wasn't until they started growing underground that they lost their sight."

"I don't believe that," said Ashley.

"Remember when we went to that cave," said Mary. "They said that blind salamanders lived in the darkness of the caves. After awhile, all the new salamanders that hatched in the cave were blind because they never saw light. It's got to work the same way for potatoes."

Ashley just sighed. She knew that potatoes had never grown on trees.

Dad continued, "So Noggin let the stick borrow her pet potato, named Spud. Stick and Spud got closer and closer to the mysterious, red glowing stuff."

"I know what it is!" said Mary. "It's lava and they were standing on a volcano."

"You're exactly right," said Dad. "And what do you think they discovered when Stick and Spud got really close to the lava?"

"Fire!" blurted Mary.

"No," Dad shook his head. "Not quite. The first thing they discovered was the baked potato. The stick saw that it made Spud smell so yummy and feel so soft, Stick decided it wanted to smell and feel the same way. Stick put its tip right into the lava."

"The lava was so hot it caught Stick on fire. Noggin knew just what to do. She needed to race back to the glacier and put the hot fire on the cold ice. As she came down the path, Noggin and Stick bumped right into the bearasaurus."

"The smell of singed bearasaurus fur filled the air. Stick had run right into the paw of the great peeping bearasaurus. It started peeping and dancing around. The bearasaurus started huffing and puffing on its huge paw."

"Finally, the fire went out. Surprisingly the fire didn't burn the bearasaurus that badly. Nevertheless, it did burn up the thorn. The last little bit crumbled into ashes and fell to the ground. Noggin and Stick had cured the bearasaurus."

"Noggin suddenly had an idea. She asked the bearasaurus to put out the fire on Stick. The bearasaurus huffed and puffed. At first, Stick burned a little brighter. A not so known fact about the bearasaurus is that when they huff and puff they also slobber."

"That's what put out the fire. So of course, Noggin made another great discovery, the fire extinguisher. Eventually, every cave family had a bearasaurus hanging on a wall just in case that newfangled contraption called fire got out of hand. Of course, it had to be invented all over again when the bearasaurus went extinct."

"Maybe that's why Smokey Bear puts out fires," suggested Mom. "He might be part bearasaurus."

All the children laughed.

"Hey, I'm supposed to be the funny one," objected Dad. "So what did you learn?"

"I learned something," said Michael. "Never sit on the front row if a bearasaurus is the speaker. You'll get covered in slobber."

## Chapter 7
## The Handsome Prince

"I'm still worried about Noggin," said Mary. "She can't find her way back to her family."

"I'd be more concerned about the volcano," said Ashley.

"I would agree with Mary this time," said Michael. "There's not much she can do about the volcano. It would be best if she could find her family. Maybe she could warn them. Maybe if she had a race car time machine…"

"It's not that kind of story," interrupted Ashley. "Now, if she met a handsome caveman prince he could rescue her and become her boyfriend."

"I'm too young to have a boyfriend," objected Mary.

"You'd better take this story back over before there is a riot," Mom said to Dad.

"Yes," agreed Dad as he tossed another log on the campfire. "Noggin was very worried about finding her family too. Since she didn't have a race car time machine, she had to find another solution. And she would need to be rescued, for she had decided to go back down the path."

"She didn't get too far before both her and Stick slipped on a rock. Her feet dangled off the side of the mountain. Below her were jagged rocks. Noggin managed to grab the strange rock at the top of the path."

"The bearasaurus heard her scream. He came running to rescue her, just as she had saved him from the thorn in the paw. He was able to reach Stick because it fell on the side of the path nearest him. The bearasaurus couldn't speak Caveman, so he had to use motions. He moved his arms back and forth."

"It reminded Noggin of when her mom rocked her to sleep as a baby. Noggin shook her head no. She didn't want to take a nap. The bearasaurus let out a heavy bear sigh. Next, he pointed to a leg and started shaking it."

"If your leg itches, use Stick to scratch it," Noggin told the bearasaurus as she pointed to the walking stick.

"The bearasaurus didn't understand a word Noggin said, but noticed her pointing at the stick. The bearasaurus also pointed at the stick and then made it rock back and forth. Then he pointed at Noggin."

“Noggin nodded, ‘I get it. You’re telling me to rock my legs back and forth like the stick.’ She started swinging her legs. The bear nodded yes excitedly. So Noggin swung right back onto the path. The strange part was that the swinging rock and the rock it was attached to had slipped down the volcano a little bit. Above it two rocks separated. One now curved off to the left and the other to the right.”

“Noggin scrambled off to the left to join Stick and the bearasaurus. Where the rocks had split, she could see into the volcano. Rushing rivers of red lava boiled beneath her. The bearasaurus motioned for Noggin to follow him.”

“Now, I might point out,” said Dad, “That Noggin would later learn the name of the bearasaurus. His name was Prince and he certainly was quite handsome by bearasaurus standards. If you don’t believe me, ask a lady bearasaurus.”

“Dad!” interrupted Ashley, “Are you telling me that Noggin was rescued by a handsome Prince?”

“Exactly,” said Dad. “But he didn’t become her boyfriend, of course. Noggin was way too young to have a boyfriend, and well, Prince was a bearasaurus. Nevertheless, Prince did become her bear-friend.”

Ashley covered her eyes with her hands and shook her head, “If this is your idea of romance, it’s a miracle Mom married you.”

“Oh, Ashley,” said Mom. “Your dad is such a big teddy bearasaurus, I just can’t resist him.”

“Don’t start getting all smoochy on us,” sighed Michael.

“How did Noggin learn Prince’s name?” asked Mary. “She didn’t speak bearasaurus and Prince didn’t speak caveman.”

“Well,” said Dad, “They needed an interpreter.”

“What’s that?” asked Mary.

“It’s someone who knows both languages,” Dad explained. “The interpreter listens to what one person…”

“Or bearasaurus,” interrupted Mary.

“Or bearasaurus,” Dad continued. “Listens to what a person says and repeats it to the other person or bearasaurus in the language they understand.”

“Where are they going to find an interpreter?” asked Mary.

“The bearasaurus motioned for Noggin to follow him. They walked along a narrow path around the mountain and near the very top. They stopped at a large nest made of tree branches. Stick recognized one of his cousins. They were very glad to see each other.”

"What lived in the nest?" asked Mary.

"It was a giant, prehistoric bird-like, reptile-like creature called a parrot-dactyl."

"Parrot-dactyl?" questioned Michael. "Don't you mean pterodactyl? You know, the giant flying reptiles. Some had wingspans of over thirty feet."

"So that's over five Bugmi feet," said Ashley.

"Very good," said Mom. "It's good to see you use those division skills."

"Tell us about the parrot-dactyl, Dad," Mary said eagerly.

"A parrot-dactyl is a short way of saying parrot pterodactyl. That's why the word pterodactyl begins with a silent *p* now," explained Dad.

"Do not ever write that in a science paper, kids," warned Mom. "Now, if you're doing creative writing, maybe."

"Hey!" objected Dad. "I'm just telling the facts. Now, Parrot-dactyls make very fine interpreters."

"Can they talk, like parrots?" asked Mary.

"Who do you think taught parrots to talk?" asked Dad.

"Parrot-dactyls?" guessed Mary.

"You're smart, just like Noggin," said Dad.

"Yes, parrot-dactyls could talk. That's why the bearasaurus led Noggin to the nest. To Prince, everything Noggin said sounded like caveman gibberish."

"What's gibberish?" asked Ashley.

"It's nonsense talk," explained Dad.

"You know," said Michael. "Like when you get together and talk with your friends. It's all gibberish."

"Can we get a parrot-dactyl for Ashley?" asked Mary.

## Chapter 8
## The Parrot-dactyl Flight

Dad continued with the story, "As soon as Noggin, Stick, and Prince the bearasaurus reached the parrot-dactyl's nest, there was a loud rumbling on the mountain. Everything began to shake. The parrot-dactyl saw her guests and stuck her long beaked head out of her nest."

"She scooped the bearasaurus right up. This terrified Noggin and she started running back down the path. She could hear the loud flapping parrot-dactyl wings above her head. Suddenly, the mountain shook again. This made Noggin fall to the ground. She looked up as the parrot-dactyl swooped down and grabbed Stick."

"As soon as the parrot-dactyl flew off, Noggin noticed something strange. The flying reptile had not eaten the bearasaurus. In fact, Prince was riding on the back of the parrot-dactyl. He was waving for Noggin to join him."

"The mountain rumbled again. Part of the path above her tumbled into the fiery lava. As the ground shook again, it started to crack. The path below her now had a huge gap. Inside the gap was more fiery lava. Noggin was trapped."

"Oh no!" cried Mary. "I hope she was wearing sun-screen. I wouldn't want to get sunburned."

"You can't get sunburned from the ground," said Michael.

"Oh no!" sighed Mary. "And they don't make ground-screen."

“They did back then,” said Dad. “They called it mud. But Noggin didn’t need it. Being so very bright, she now knew what the parrot-dactyl was up to. She wasn’t trying to hurt anyone. She was trying to save them from the volcano.”

“Now, it takes a parrot-dactyl with a thirty foot wingspan a distance to turn around. It was now coming in for another approach. Stick was firmly gripped between the parrot-dactyl’s strong talons.”

“Noggin reached out her arms. She grabbed Stick as the parrot-dactyl swooped down. Noggin looked down as the path she had just been standing on crumbled into the volcano. Soon, Noggin was gliding like a bobcat.”

“Gliding like a bobcat?” questioned Michael. “Bobcats can’t fly.”

“I meant to say, gliding like a golden eagle,” corrected Dad. “The parrot-dactyl landed a safe distance from the volcano. This gave them all a chance to talk. The bearasaurus began by telling Noggin his name. He also stated that he was very handsome and modest by bearasaurus standards. He invited her to ask any lady bearasaurus to verify the truth. The parrot-dactyl translated from Bearasaurus to Caveman.”

“Having established that the bearasaurus was indeed a handsome Prince, Noggin began to tell her story. The parrot-dactyl and Prince were moved by the romance between the far-sighted turtles and the boulder. They were tense about the race against the speeding glacier. They were glad the rabbits finally stopped singing.

“Signing bunnies always bug me,” said the parrot-dactyl

“That of course led to the discussion of the lost tribe. They were saddened by Noggin getting lost from her family. They wanted to do anything they could to help.”

“Noggin was very glad to hear that. As it turned out, Prince knew exactly where the tunnel came out. He had hibernated there one winter. It didn’t work out so well with all the traffic coming through the tunnel.”

“The parrot-dactyl, whose name was Polly, offered to fly them there. Prince, Noggin, and Stick climbed onto the back of Polly and they were quickly airborne. As they flew, they noticed something about the volcano. More of the mountain had crumbled into the lava. It was about to spill over into the valley below them.”

“That was very bad news,” Dad continued, “For it was the valley that was at the end of the tunnel. Noggin wasn’t the only Bugmi about to discover fire. If the lava reached them, it would be very bad.”

“No!” cried Mary. “She just found her family. Nothing bad should happen to them.”

“It’s all right Mary,” comforted her mom. “Your dad won’t let anything bad happen to them.” She glanced at her husband. “In fact, something good better happen real quickly or someone is going to have nightmares.”

Dad didn’t seem to get the message as he continued, “In fact, it got much worse.”

Mom sighed and shook her head.

“Everyone, back away from the campfire,” warned Mary. “I don’t want our family to get burned.”

“Mary, there’s no lava in our campfire,” said Michael.

“Although we had that old barbecue grill that had lava rocks in it. It used to get very, very hot!” said Ashley.

“Mom!” cried Mary.

“You’re not helping,” said Mom. “Do you want a little sister with nightmares keeping you up all night?”

“No ma’am,” sighed Ashley. “Remember how good those hamburgers tasted on that grill. Lava is our friend.” Ashley tried to comfort Mary.

“You were about to say it would get much worse,” Michael said to Dad with great interest.

“I’ll try to make it quick and get to the good part,” Dad nodded at Mom.

“Skip to the part where the Bugmi tribe becomes s’mores,” suggested Ashley.

“No!” cried Mary.

“Nobody became s’mores,” said Dad.

“Now you took all the suspense out of it,” sighed Ashley.

“No he didn’t” said Mary, “but I hope he does real soon.”

“Okay,” said Dad. “First for the bad news, not only were the Bugmies in the valley, all the other cavemen were there as well. If it had just been the tribe, Polly could have given them rides out of the valley in time.”

“Noggin had Polly fly all around the volcano. She was hoping to spot a quick escape route. There wasn’t one. But as they flew around the back side of the volcano, Noggin quickly got an idea. It was an idea that would save her whole family.”

“You can thank me later,” smiled Mary.

## Chapter 9
## U-Crainian Cranes

"Noggin asked Polly if she knew any cranes," Dad began to explain Noggin's plan to save her family from the volcano.

"Polly said she knew a family of giant cranes. She turned and flapped off to their marsh. Fortunately, Polly spoke U-cranian. That was the language of the cranes."

"Dad," corrected Michael, "Ukraine is a country in Eastern Europe. It's not a language spoken by cranes."

"Do you understand Ukrainian?" asked Dad.

"No," sighed Michael. He knew what was coming next.

"Do you understand when cranes talk?" asked Dad.

"I've never heard cranes talk," said Michael.

"Then why are you so sure they don't speak U-cranian, especially when talking to parrot-dactyls?"

"Stop interrupting him," said Mary. "The volcano is about to explode and the Bugmies might become s'mores."

May I have another s'more?" asked Ashley. "All this story telling is making me hungry."

"Sure," said Mom as she reached for a marshmallow roasting stick, "but, no more after this. It's getting late."

"Hear that, Dad," said Mary. "It's too late for the Bugmies to become s'mores."

"I never said the Bugmies were going to become s'mores," defended Dad. "Now I don't even remember who mentioned that."

"Never mind," said Mary.

"Yes," agreed Ashley, "just continue with the U-cranian parrot, while I enjoy my nice, toasty s'more."

"Meanwhile," Dad continued with the story. "Back in the valley, some Bugmies were riding around on the back of Shelly the brontosaurus. Oof sniffed the air. 'What that strange smell?' asked Oof. Ash sniffed the air. 'Smell nice and toasty. I like. Whatever it is I like some more.'"

“How is this helping save the Bugmies?” asked Mary. “Meanwhile, what is happening with the giant cranes? Go back to that meanwhile.”

“Oh yes,” said Dad, “I was just thinking about having another s’more myself. Ashley’s does smell nice and toasty.”

“I’ll fix it,” said Mom. “Just keep telling the story.”

“Meanwhile, back at the marsh, Noggin was explaining her plan. She told Polly. The parrot-dactyl translated it into U-cranian. She also translated it into bearasaurus so Prince wouldn’t feel left out.”

“They all agreed it was their best hope to save the Bugmies. The giant cranes flew back to the valley with Polly and her passengers. It was pretty easy to spot the Bugmies on Shelly’s back. As soon as the parrot-dactyl was on the ground, Noggin hopped off. She ran to her family.”

“The Bugmies were amazed. ‘What you call that?’ cried Wah.”

“Noggin was about to say walking, but it was so much faster than she had walked. She decided to give it a different name. Since the grass she was on made a ‘run, run’ sound with every step she started calling it run, run or run for short. It’s a good thing she didn’t run on the patch of ground to her left or she would have called it flibberglippen. Can you imagine a plane landing on a flibberglippenway?”

“Anyway, Oof asked, ‘How you do that?’ Well, Noggin wanted to teach them to run, just in case her plan didn’t work. But you have to walk before you run. In the distance, another rumble from the volcano reminded her that there simply wasn’t time to explain at the moment. I mean she would have to teach about toes, then feet, then legs. There were just too many discoveries to cover in such a short time.”

“Hurry, Dad!” said Mary. “The volcano is about to blow up.”

“Well,” said Dad “She had all the Bugmies slide off the back of the Shelly. Next, Noggin and Prince the bearasaurus gathered up some thick vines. They slipped them under Shelly’s belly.”

"Once they were done, Polly shouted some orders in U-cranian. The giant birds grabbed the ends of the vines with their beaks. Their huge wings began to flap. Soon, they were lifting Shelly into the sky."

"They sat Shelly down very gently at the base of the volcano. Noggin was right behind them riding on Polly's back. Prince and Noggin began to tie the vines together. They worked very hurriedly."

"The ground was shaking. The volcano was rumbling. Smoke was beginning to spew out of its top. There wasn't a moment to waste."

"Noggin grabbed the end and raced up the strange stone pathway," said Dad.

"The one with the offset rocks and the strange flap at the top?" asked Michael.

"That's the one," said Dad. "At the top of the path, Noggin tied the vine to the flapping rock. Next, she raced back down and climbed up to the top of Shelly's neck. She commanded the brontosaurus to move forward."

"The vines began to tighten as Shelly tugged. The flapping rock began to be pulled down the mountain. As it did, the rocky pathway split into two paths. 'Forward, go!' Noggin encouraged the brontosaurus to pull."

"Wait!" said Michael, "Are you saying that there was a giant zipper built into the volcano?"

"Yes," said Dad. "This was before they had the more modern Velcro volcanoes. Before that there were the old fashioned lace-up volcanoes. It's a good thing it was the zipper model. Noggin would have never got it un-laced in time."

"What happened next?" asked Mary excitedly.

"Shelly tugged and the volcano unzipped. The lava poured forth," explained Dad.

"Oh no!" cried Mary. "You promised the Bugmies weren't going to become s'more."

"That was the beauty of Noggin's plan," explained Dad. "The lava wasn't pouring down into the valley with all the cavemen. It was flowing down into the valley that was filling up with the speedy glacier."

## Chapter 10
## Getting Steamed

"That was close," said Mary. "I'm glad my plan worked."

"Noggin's plan," corrected Ashley. "So what happened when the lava met the glacier?"

"All that ice started to melt," explained Dad. "That was the end of the speeding glacier. Steam filled the air. The hissing sound of the lava hitting the ice scared Shelly. She bolted out running. That took Noggin by surprise. She slid right off the back of the brontosaurus."

"All the steam made it very difficult to see. Noggin had to walk blindly toward where she thought Prince and Polly were. Then Noggin began to notice something. Her feet were getting very cold. She got down on her knees and felt around."

"Suddenly, her hand got wet. She turned around and crawled some more. A few feet later, her hand was wet again. Then the ground she was on began to tip as she moved. Noggin slowly began to realize that she was on a floating piece of ice. Not only that, but the ice was melting."

"Noggin cried out for help. She could hear Polly's loud flapping wings above her. The problem was that the parrot-dactyl couldn't see anything. In fact, the steam and smoke from the volcano were even worse up in the air."

"Noggin cried out again. This time she heard a splash. 'Help!' Noggin continued to cry out. The splashing sound grew nearer. It was a please-see-her-asaur."

"Don't you mean a plesiosaur? They were a reptile that lived in the water and had fins instead of legs," explained Michael.

"It was Oof's idea," explained Dad. "He had found Stick and asked Stick to lead him to Noggin. At first he didn't know how to walk, but of course Stick was a walking stick. Oof learned quickly. Polly saw them walking toward the volcano. She had flown over the valley to make sure the Bugmies were ok."

Stick had Oof hold up the stick and Polly scoop them up. Soon, Oof was gliding like a bobcat, I mean golden eagle. Oof suggest that the cranes grab a please-see-her-asaur from a nearby lake and take it to the melted glacier."

"Luckily, Oof had been a please-see-her-asaur captain when he was younger. The new models of please-see-her-asaurs had echo location. Sort of like submarines have sonar."

"Just like dolphins," said Ashley. "We read about that in science."

"You read about please-see-her-asaurs in science?" asked Mary.

"No," said Ashley. "We read about dolphins and echo location. They can find things by making a sound. The sound bounces off objects. The amount of time it takes for the echo to reach them lets them know how far away an object is."

"So," said Dad. "Oof captained the please-see-her-asaur and rescued Noggin. It was just in time too, for that chunk of ice had melted down to the size of an ice cube. It was just big enough for her to stand on with one toe. It was even the pinky toe at that."

"And the dad was the hero once again," concluded Michael.

"How did you know that was what I was going to say?" asked Dad.

"All your stories end with the dad being the hero," said Ashley.

Mary gave her dad a hug, "You are my hero."

"Wait, is that the end of the story?" asked Mom.

"You want more?" asked Dad.

"I'd like to know what happened when everyone found out that Noggin saved them from the volcano," suggested Mom.

"Well, of course, she was a big hero too," said Dad. "All the cavemen were very grateful. The whole Bugmi tribe was once again accepted. In fact they were given a new name. From that day on they were called the Like'em tribe because everyone liked them."

"Oof ran for chief in the next election. Noggin ran his campaign and did a brilliant job. Oof easily won. Arp discovered it was much easier to cook with fire. She wrote a very successful cookbook. Perhaps you've heard of s'mores? That was on page 35 in the dessert section. Wah started a band. Having gotten his inspiration from being hit by a rock, he called it the Tumbling Stones."

“They had several big hits. In fact, that’s where we get the term “hit song’ because they started every song using rolling rocks. It became much less painful to be in the band when they discovered you didn’t need to be hit by a rock to start singing.”

“What about Ash?” asked Ashley.

“She became very wealthy,” said Dad.

“All right!” said Ashley.

“Working for her brilliant little sister Noggin,” Dad continued.

“Never in a million years,” objected Ashley.

“Just kidding,” said Dad. “She became a real estate developer and sold lakeside lots around the melted glacier lake. She did pretty well for herself.”

“Finally, Noggin went on to make many more brilliant discoveries. She discovered the wheel, followed by the toe cast for toes that get ran over by wheels. Noggin was famous for many things, but what mattered to her the most was that she found her family again.

“You can sure make up some crazy stories, Dad,” said Michael.

“Made up?” questioned Dad.

He grabbed a vine on a tree and shook it. Two people wearing animal skins slid down the vine.

“Hey, Noggin did I make this story up?”

Noggin answered “Just a little bit. But must punch up story to make interesting. Otherwise, Oof fall asleep.”

“Oof like fun story, make Oof look smart,” nodded Oof. “Very good story.”

“I agree,” said Mom. “Your dad is almost as good a story teller as he is an inventor. Still, his stories are quite long and it’s getting late. Perhaps we should get back, now.”

“It will certainly be much, much later when we get home,” Dad laughed, “I suppose you’re right. Let’s get in the van kids.”

“Bring back shrink ray next time,” reminded Noggin. “We take care of T-rex problem for good.”

“I’ll mount it on the roof,” said Dad.

“Where’s our picnic basket? Did that bearasaurus just take it?” asked Ashley.

“I won’t make that boo-boo again,” said Mom. “I locked it in the van right after we ate dinner.”

“Hey Dad, why don’t you build your next time machine in a sports car?” asked Michael.

“Do you know what that would do to our insurance rates, Son?” asked Dad.

The family piled into the mini-van. They waved goodbye to Oof and Noggin. The van began to make a whistling sound as it slowly lifted off the ground. Dad pushed a red button. The van began to spin very rapidly. It quickly became a blur. Suddenly, it disappeared back to the future.

# Thomas Jefferson and the Louisiana Purchase

Thomas Jefferson

***On April 30, 1803*** *the United States purchased the rights to the Louisiana territory from France. Napoleon Bonaparte, the emperor of France needed money to fight a war with Britain. He had obtained the territory from Spain three years earlier. U. S. president, Thomas Jefferson sent representatives to France. They were instructed to try to purchase New Orleans. Napoleon responded with an even bigger plan.*

Napoleon Bonaparte

*The result was the purchase of territory that would become parts of 14 states. Having acquired such a vast territory, President Jefferson was anxious to explore the new addition to the United States. His good friend and personal secretary, Meriwether Lewis, would lead the expedition. The expedition was also known as the Corps of Discovery. Meriwether Lewis would be joined with William Clark to explore what would later be known as the Lewis and Clark trail.*

### Planning With the President

"We'll announce it to the country on July 4th," said the president.

"I guess you could call it a birthday present, then," smiled his friend, Meriwether as he looked at the piece of paper.

"I never planned to spend fifteen million dollars for a birthday present," beamed President Jefferson.

"At 3 cents an acre, I'd say you got a good deal," said Meriwether Lewis.

"The plan was to buy the port of New Orleans. I was more than a little surprised when the delegation returned from France with a treaty to buy all of the territory. It makes me a little uneasy."

"Why is that?" asked Meriwether.

"I'm not sure the constitution allows a president to buy territory," said Jefferson. "We worked so hard to assure that states that their rights would be protected."

"Still," added Meriwether Lewis, "The port is important. When the Spanish closed it to Americans, it created a real hardship for trading. With control of the Mississippi River, you've insured farmers will have a waterway to move their goods down the river. Industry will grow and we won't be at the mercy of the Spanish or the French."

 Thomas Jefferson and Napoleon Bonaparte Pictures are Public Domain 

“That was my reasoning too,” said the president. “The good outweighs the potential risks to the constitution.”

“Aren’t you a bit intrigued with all the possibilities?”

“More than intrigued,” smiled the president. “The possibilities are unlimited. I’m a bit envious of you. I wish I could join you on your journey.”

“I’ll take good notes,” said Meriwether. “It will be just like you were there.”

“When winter sets in and I’m snug here in Washington, I’m sure I’ll be glad I’m not there.”

Meriwether smiled. He knew there was a bit a truth in the statement. He could experience harsh winter weather on the journey. Still, he knew there was much to see and learn. It was well worth the discomfort.

“Did you get the medals?” asked the president.

“Yes. But we’re also collecting other gifts for the Indians. Clark is purchasing flags, clothing, knives, tomahawks, beads, looking-glasses, paints, and handkerchiefs, and whatever else he can think of.”

“Good, good,” said the president. “Let’s try to establish as good of relationships with the natives as possible. Let them know that we want peace with them.”

“I would hate to fight our way across the land. Still, it will be good to be escorted by additional soldiers as far as the Mandan nation.”

“Let’s hope it doesn’t come to that,” said the president.

“We’ll do our best,” said Lewis.

“How is Clark coming with the rest of the preparations?” asked President Thomas Jefferson.

“William is purchasing the supplies for the expedition. I’ll start out on July 5th. I’ll meet up with him in Louisville.”

“How are the boats coming?” asked the president.

“We have three being readied. A fifty-five foot long keel boat has one sail and 22 oars. We’ll also take two open boats. We’ll keep a couple of horses following along the shore to bring back game if we need to hunt for provisions.”

“Don’t travel too far away from civilization before winter,” suggested the president.

“We plan to winter at La Charette,” answered Lewis.

It wouldn’t work out that way. The Spanish commander of the providence had not received official word that the territory would now be in control of the United States. They spent the winter on the eastern side of the Mississippi River. Lewis and Clark had a fort built. They used the time to train the men and make preparations.

The expedition party consisted of Lewis and Clark, nine young men from Kentucky, fourteen U.S. Army soldiers, two French watermen, an interpreter and hunter, and a black slave that belonged to William Clark.

A corporal and six soldiers as well as nine additional watermen would accompany them as far as the Mandan nation of Indians. They were there to assist in carrying supplies and to help in fighting off any attacks. Altogether, 45 men would begin the trip.

Meriwether Lewis also purchased a large dog for twenty dollars. The dog's name was Seaman. It was a breed called a Newfoundland. It was a very large dog. The breed is known as very good swimmers. They were bred to help fishermen.

The expedition would begin on Monday, May 14th, 1804. They traveled only four miles the first day. They would eventually travel all the way to the Pacific Ocean. It would conclude on September 23, 1806 when they reached St. Louis.

The men on the expedition kept journals. You can read about their day to day adventures. They tell about different kinds of animals and plants they discovered, such as prairie dogs. Some were even sent back to the President. Tales of their encounters with Native American tribes are detailed. They drew maps and described the land in great detail. Their journals are full of all kinds of interesting stories.

You can even explore the Lewis and Clark trail yourself. Their journey is marked out in several places with special parks and exhibits along the way. It certainly looks quite different today than it did when Lewis and Clark passed through.

# Members of the Lewis and Clark Expedition

Meriwether Lewis

*There are many interesting stories about the members of the Lewis and Clark Expedition. Only one member of the expedition died during the trip. Charles Floyd was a relative of William Clark. Modern doctors agree he probably died of appendicitis. It was a condition that is easily cured today. Doctors did not know how to treat it in 1804. He would have likely died no matter where he was.*

William Clark

*Captains Clark and Lewis split the party for awhile on the trip back. They wanted to explore more land. Two Blackfeet Indians were killed while trying to steal weapons from the group of men led by Captain Lewis. They traveled 100 miles the next day to get away from the Blackfeet.*

## Pierre Cruzatte

One member of the expedition got shot. Meriwether Lewis found out the hard way that it was not safe to hunt with Pierre Cruzatte. He was a member of the expedition. He was blind in one eye and nearsighted in the other. Pierre thought Lewis was an elk from a distance. He fired a shot.

Meriwether Lewis was struck in the leg. The bullet passed through. Captain Lewis was fortunate the bullet didn't strike the bone. He was still in great pain.

At first Captain Lewis assumed he had been shot by Cruzatte. He was aware of the hunter's poor eyesight. The captain was wearing brown leather. He began calling out to Cruzatte. The hunter didn't answer.

Next, Lewis reasoned he had been shot by Indians hiding in the woods. He ordered everyone back to the boats. They began to search the woods. Meriwether Lewis had to return to the boats when his leg began to get stiff.

The men came back and reported that they had not seen any Indians. They did find Cruzatte. He said he had shot an elk. The captain knew that Pierre would not intentionally shoot him.

The captain was in great pain and he had a fever. The men were not sure he would live. The next day, Captain Clark's group met up with them. Captain Clark's joy of reuniting with the rest of the party quickly turned to great concern. Meriwether Lewis did begin to recover after a few days. It would be weeks before he could easily walk.

 Portraits by Charles Willson Peale, Public Domain 

## York

William Clark owned a slave. They had grown up together. The slave, named York, was also on the expedition. He was the only African-American on the expedition. He was a skilled hunter and a valuable member of the team. He experienced more freedom on the expedition then most slaves.

Many Indian tribes were comforted to see a dark skinned man with the white explorers. He most likely eased tensions with the Indians on many occasions. He was well respected by the men on the expedition and treated as an equal.

When the expedition was over, it was difficult for York to continue as a slave. He asked for his freedom several times. He wanted to rejoin his wife who was owned by a man in Louisville, Kentucky.

William Clark did let him visit his wife once for a few weeks. All the other members of the expedition received land and money for serving. York did not. He was considered William Clark's property.

There are many stories about what eventually happened to York. Most likely he escaped slavery. One historian believes he went to live among the Crow tribe.

## Sacagawea

Sacagawea is one of the more famous members of the expedition. She joined up with them at Fort Mandan. Her husband was a Frenchman named Charbonneau. Sacagawea was probably about sixteen when she joined the expedition. William Clark nicknamed her Janey.

Sacagawea had a baby named John Baptiste during the expedition. It had to be difficult being a new mother and an explorer at the same time. She was very helpful. Many people assume she was a guide for the trip, but most of the places they traveled were unfamiliar to her.

She did help as an interpreter among other Indian tribes. She also had knowledge of edible roots and other foods that helped feed the members. Indian war parties never included women. The sight of Sacagawea helped Indian tribes realize that the expedition was peaceful.

She had been kidnapped from her tribe by another tribe when she was about twelve years old. During the trip Lewis needed to trade for some horses to cross the Rocky Mountains. There was great excitement among a tribe of Shoshone at the sight of Sacagawea. The captain asked Sacagawea to interpret for them. It turned out that the tribe's chief was her brother.

After the expedition, historians are unsure what happened to Sacagawea. She may have died of sickness in 1812 at about the age of 25 years old. Others think she may have lived until 1884. Her son, John Baptiste was adopted by William Clark.

## William Clark

William Clark was the younger brother of George Rogers Clark, who was once approached by Thomas Jefferson to explore the Louisiana territory before it was purchased. After the expedition, Thomas Jefferson appointed William Clark as a general over the Louisiana territory. This also made him an agent for Indian affairs. Later, William Clark was appointed as governor of the Missouri territory. He had eight children. His firstborn son was named Meriwether Lewis Clark.

## George Shannon

George Shannon was the youngest member of the expedition. He seemed very inexperienced in the beginning but became a skilled and useful member on the trip. He is most famous for a story that happened on an early part of the trip. It nearly cost him his life. You will read about his adventure in the story, *Lost on the Trail.*

# Lost on the Trail

Story and illustrations by
Brian Davis

## Vocabulary Words

asset
bluff
circumstances
expedition
massive
sinew
survival
whittling
woodsmen

Based on the journals of the members of the Lewis and Clark Expedition, we learn the story about George Shannon, who was lost in the American wilderness for several weeks. With courage and determination, he struggled to survive. His great adventure would become a part of history.

## Chapter 1
## Memories on the Trail

August 26, 1804

"Not again," sighed William Clark as he heard the news.

Two horses were missing. They had wandered away from the camp. The animals were useful in exploring the land around the river. They also carried supplies for dealing with Indians and hunting expeditions.

Captain Lewis sent two men to find the animals. George Shannon was the youngest member of the Lewis and Clark Expedition. George Drouillard had also been sent out with young George Shannon. The leader of the expedition was confident George would return in a few hours.

As the morning wore on, the two Georges decided that they could cover more ground if they split up. They agreed to meet back at the same spot by sundown. Shortly after they parted ways, George Shannon had picked up a trail. He figured he would happen upon the horses at most any time.

So intent was the young private on the trail that he lost track of time. Darkness was upon him before he realized it. There would be no return trip to the meeting spot. George Shannon realized he was now on his own. Still, he wasn't too bothered by it. He had a general sense of where the river was. He also knew he was on the trail of the horses.

He had named the two horses Frisky and Patch. It was most likely Frisky that led Patch astray. That horse seemed to always be getting into trouble. The last time it strayed, it stepped on a fur trapper's trap. Fortunately, it didn't injure Frisky. It did take out a small chunk of its left, front hoof. That made for a distinctive hoof print. That's why George was so sure he was on the right path.

That wasn't the only reason he didn't want to give up and return to the boats. He also wanted to prove he could be an asset to the expedition. It was tough being the youngest. The more experienced woodsmen teased him about his lack of survival skills. Captain Lewis understood this and gave George opportunities to prove himself.

George climbed a rock. He found a shallow cave that could provide some shelter for the night. With a piece of flint and steel George was able to start a small fire. It was August and the nights didn't get too cool. Still, the flames would keep wild animals away.

He pulled a piece of the dried meat from a pouch. It was enough for tonight, but by morning, he would want some fresh game. He hadn't planned to be out overnight. A short trip into the woods often led to the retrieval of the horses.

George rested on the rock. He kept his rifle on his lap. He would have preferred to stay awake to keep an eye on things. He was tired after hiking through the woods and across open prairies all day.

His eyes grew heavy. George let out a big yawn. Before drifting off to sleep, George rolled a thick log onto the fire. It should be enough to keep the flame going until morning.

The flames would keep animals away, but they might also draw the attention of men. There were Sioux, Maha, and Pawnee tribes in the area. The native people had been helpful and friendly for the most part. George wouldn't mind having a little company if any happened to stop by. They may even help find the horses.

George would have no such luck. He was alone. He listened to the sounds of the night. Occasionally, he heard the screech of an owl, or the yipping of a pack of coyotes. When he first joined the expedition, the sounds would have bothered him. Now, he was used to them. It was actually calming to him.

Young George thought about how his life had changed over the last few months. He greatly admired Captain Lewis. He was after all handpicked by the President Jefferson to head up the expedition. When the captain chose George to come along, he was greatly honored.

The captain overlooked George's youth and inexperience. He saw potential in the young man. He was intelligent, loyal, hardworking, and didn't complain about doing the menial tasks. In fact, George carried a kit of needles and thread called a "housewife". He was always mending socks and clothing for the other men. It was menial work, but George was just grateful he could be of help.

As George chewed the last bit of dried meat for the night, he remembered the first time he had met Seaman. George didn't expect the log to give way as he crossed over the rain swollen stream. It was normally only knee deep. The spring rains had turned it into a torrent.

George flailed helplessly as he was carried along by the strong current. He choked on the water, gasping for air. When he first saw the massive ball of fur coming toward him, he thought it was a bear. He still wasn't sure when the teeth gripped the sleeve of his jacket.

The raging stream was wearing him out fast. He thought of all the stories of people, even good swimmers who had drowned in these exact circumstances. He wasn't sure which way he preferred to die, drowning or being eaten by a bear.

In reality, he had little choice. It was a battle between the river and the animal. George just didn't have strength to exert his will. When he felt his knees drag under the water, he knew the beast had won.

Suddenly, a hand reached out and caught his arm. He was pulled to shore. That was his first encounter with Meriwether Lewis. It was also his first encounter with the massive breed of dog called a Newfoundland.

George rewarded Seaman's heroics with some dried, but now soggy, beef from his pocket. The dog seemed to think the life of the young man for a strip of beef was a fair exchange. The dog and George became fast friends.

## Chapter 2
## Teepee on the Trail

August 28, 1804

George let out a sigh of relief at the sight. The two horses grazed under the shade of the large cottonwood trees. They saw him, but they weren't alarmed. The horses were used to George Shannon. He brushed them and spoke softly to them every evening.

"You are nothing but trouble," George said to the horse he called Frisky as he snapped a rope onto the halter.

The horse shook its head up and down as if in agreement. George snapped another rope onto Patches. The second horse nuzzled its head in George's chest. She was glad to see her human friend. He always brought her a treat.

He didn't have much. In fact, he hadn't found anything to hunt. He found a berry patch. It was a nice addition to the dried meat. George had eaten his fill and stuck a few extras in his pocket. It was a meager treat, but Patches didn't seem to mind.

"Don't eat all my food," said George when the horse tried to pick his pocket for more. "You can always eat grass if you're hungry. I don't have that option."

George looked over the land. After getting his bearings from the position of the sun, he decided on the direction to travel. He would have to take the horses back to the river. From there, he would need to catch up with the rest of the explorers.

"We'd better be moving. I'd reckon the rest of them are already upstream a bit. I can't believe the two of you wandered so far away. There are patches of grass all over the place."

Frisky whinnied a reply.

"I see," said George. "You wanted to get out of working for a few days. Why is it that every time you get out of working, you cause so much more work for me? You made me trek through this wilderness for days trying to find you. I hope you appreciate what I had to go through."

The horse shook its head as if answering no.

George planted his hands on his hips and stood up straight. "If that's what you think of me, then maybe you should start earning your keep right now."

With that, George pulled himself up onto the back to Frisky. "Now, we'll see whose turn it is to put in a little work."

Patches followed in line as George rode Frisky back down the path. George Shannon kept his eyes open for any sign of the other George. It had been several days since they had last seen each other. He hoped to find him sitting by a campfire roasting a rabbit or two.

George had not eaten anything but dried meat and wild grapes the whole day. He had just finished the last bit of meat. He had shot at a few rabbits and missed. It reminded him of a recent hunting trip with some of the other men.

He had spotted a wild pheasant. George carefully took aim, shot, and missed as the bird flew off. One of the men stumbled onto the bird's nest and chased down a young bird. The man offered to hold it while George shot it.

"Just to build your confidence," teased the man.

"What if he hits you instead?" asked another hunter.

"I should be safe. He's never hit anything before," laughed the first man.

George didn't think it was funny at the time. He still didn't think it was funny. He knew the truth was he wasn't much of a hunter. He was getting better at target practice. It was just harder to hit a moving target like a rabbit or a deer.

His supply of bullets was getting low. He felt in the leather pouch tied at his waist. Only two small lead balls remained. He would have to make them count.

Clouds were rolling in from the northwest. George didn't want to be caught on the grassy prairie during a storm. At first he thought about hurrying to the river. Then he remembered how the rivers swelled during heavy rains. He would be safer from a flash flood if he stayed where he was. He had seen the water rise several feet in an hour during a heavy rainfall.

As George studied the sky he almost missed what was on the ground. Frisky didn't miss it. The horse stepped around the large lump as it climbed a hill. The change in direction caught George's attention. He looked down and saw the large buffalo hides.

When he slipped off the horse, George noticed the poles. Now, he knew what he was looking at. It was part of an abandoned teepee from the Sioux tribe. He was pleased to see it. The teepee would provide good shelter from the storm if he could get it set up in time.

He had one problem. He had never set up a teepee. He hadn't even watched the Sioux put up teepees. He wasn't sure one person could do it by themselves.

The poles and hides were heavy. Then he realized the horses were strong. George ran to the top of the hill. He was pleased with what he saw. A small grove of trees was ahead. His idea should work.

The horses lugged the poles and hides to the trees. George wouldn't make a teepee, but he would make a storm shelter. He lodged the poles between branches and the tree trunk.

Next, George tossed hides over the poles. He used his knife to quickly carve four stakes. A rock was used to pound them into the ground. There were enough sinew straps to tie the hides to the stakes.

The first drops of rain began to fall as George tied down the last corner of his tent. He tied the horses to the trunk of the tree. George didn't want to spend the next few days chasing them down again. George listened to the patter of rain on the hide with gratefulness for the protection of the tent. He admired the colorful paintings the Sioux had made on the buffalo hide.

## Chapter 3
## The Snake Snack

August 29, 1804

It wasn't long before George and the horses reached the river. He was relieved to see the water, but he was disappointed that the expedition was nowhere to be found. He calculated that the boats couldn't be more than a day ahead of him. Hopefully, they would camp somewhere and explore the land. It would give him a chance to catch up.

There was a bluff ahead. Perhaps he could climb up it and look up the river. Any smoke from a camp would be welcome. Even an Indian camp would be a welcome sight. Part of the mission of the expedition was to establish peaceful relationships with the native tribes.

They sought out tribal chiefs to meet. Captain Lewis brought gifts such as tobacco, corn, medals, articles of clothing, and kettles. If George had been with the expedition, he would have had the opportunity to share a meal of a plump, cooked dog. That may not have sounded that good to George normally, but he was getting very hungry.

He had two bullets left and wanted to make them count. If he could shoot a larger animal, like a deer, he could dry some meat and have plenty to eat. He also figured it would be easer to hit a larger target.

George climbed the bluff. It gave a beautiful view of the river below. He looked up and down the river. There was no sign of the expedition. He scanned the horizon. There was no smoke from campfires. George was afraid he was farther behind than he thought.

He led Frisky and Patch down the path. Suddenly, he froze. There ahead of him was a young doe. It was coming to the river for a drink. This was the opportunity George had been waiting for. He lifted the gun to his shoulder. It contained the next to last, precious, lead ball. He carefully took aim.

Just as he pulled the trigger, Frisky came up to George and nudged him in the back. The gun went off and the deer scampered off into the bushes that lined the river.

The blast of the gun scared Frisky at the same time. The horse reared up on its hind legs. George turned and saw that the horse was about to come down on him. He jumped out of the way. Frisky took off down the path toward the river.

Patches stood a few yards back. The second horse looked just as surprised as George at the behavior of Frisky. Then George noticed something on the trail.

He moved a little closer. George carefully lowered his gun to the object. He nudged it with the barrel of the gun. It was motionless. George moved closer.

It was what he thought it was. A prairie rattlesnake lay dead on the path. Frisky had trampled it. Perhaps that explained the horse's strange behavior.

George pulled out his knife. He cut the head off the snake. He buried the head to protect anyone coming along the path. Even the fangs of a dead rattlesnake can deliver venom to someone stepping on the head.

The snake would make a good meal. George picked it up and continued on down the path. He wanted to catch up to Frisky and make sure the animal had not been bitten. George kept his eyes open for more snakes as he approached the river. The thought of being bitten and having no one to help him was very concerning.

George felt a chill run down his spine when he got to the bottom of the hill. Frisky was lying on the grass next to the path. When the horse saw George, it stood up. George scratched the horse's head lovingly. He appreciated that the horse tried to save his life.

He led the horse out of the taller grass. Frisky favored its right, front hoof. That was not a good sign. George studied it carefully. There didn't appear to be a snake bite. There were no puncture wounds, bleeding, or swelling.

The horse must have injured itself as it ran down the path. George decided to build a fire and let the horse rest. It would give George time to cook the snake. Frisky appeared to be uncomfortable. The horse had a slight limp as it grazed among the tall grass.

George didn't mind the rest either as he watched the snake cook over the fire. It didn't look to be the most appetizing meal, but it was food. That was getting pretty scarce. He occasionally found a berry bush, but that was about all.

The horses were starting to drift too far away from the fire. George didn't want to lose them again. He had already gone through several days of trouble and worry to find them. He walked toward the horses.

They were making their way to the river to get a drink. As he got to the muddy river bank, he noticed all kind of hoof prints. He was trying to match them up with the animals that could have made them. Suddenly, he noticed prints that were immediately recognizable.

There were human footprints in the muddy riverbank. He knew they couldn't have been more than a day old. George was very excited. He thought he was close to the expedition and could maybe catch up today if he hurried.

When the horses had drank their fill of water, George turned back to the fire.

"No!" he shouted as he ran back to his lunch. "Get away from there!"

It was too late. The red tail of the fox was the last he saw of his snake. The animal had stolen it, stick and all. George was very disappointed. His stomach ached for a cooked meal.

He comforted himself with the thought that he would soon catch up with the expedition.

He picked out a trail up the river. George was anxious to cover the miles to catch up with the group. The expedition often traveled about eight miles a day. George would have to keep moving.

After about an hour on the trail George was beginning to realize something. Frisky was in a lot of pain. The horse bravely tried to continue, but the pace was too quick. George had to make a decision. He could stop and let Frisky heal for a few days or he could continue with only Patches.

It was a difficult decision. In part, he would have failed in his mission to bring back both horses. Still, if he couldn't catch up with the expedition, the horses would be of no use to them anyway. It was possible that Frisky would still be limping a few days from now. Then there may be no hope of finding the others.

George stopped. He looked Frisky in the eyes. Maybe some Indians would find the horse and nurse it back to health. That was the best George could hope for. He pulled off the harness and the rest of the load it was carrying. He had already moved most of his gear to the back of Patches.

Frisky seemed to understand that it was slowing down their progress. The horse neighed softly and turned away. George held the rope tied to Patches firmly. He didn't want the second horse to follow Frisky. Patches didn't even try. George figured the horse was anxious to find the expedition too.

## Chapter 4
## Hungry Enough

September 9, 1804

The hunger was beginning to take over. George had eaten nothing but wild grapes for days. With no bullets, his gun was useless for hunting. Weak from not eating, George rested in the shade. He picked up his knife and started whittling on a stick. It was the end of another hard day traveling.

He watched Patches graze on some grass. George wished he could eat grass like a horse. The thought brought back a memory of his father. After a hard day's work, his father would come in the house and bellow, "What's for dinner. I'm hungry enough to eat a horse."

George smiled and laughed. Then a thought struck him. Patches suddenly looked very appetizing. That horse would certainly provide George with a lot of meat. George rapidly shook his head no, trying to drive the thought out of his head.

The horse belonged to the Expedition. His job was to find the horses, not eat them. He couldn't imagine Captain Lewis being too pleased to learn that the only remaining horse he had been set out to retrieve had become a meal. George felt it was his own fault he hadn't caught up with the rest of the men in the last fourteen days. He must have been moving too slowly. George felt a little guilty about stopping while there was still daylight.

George focused once again on his whittling. He was carving a little doll. He figured he could give it to some Indian child along the way. President Jefferson had encouraged them to show acts of kindness to the native people.

The wood was much harder than what he normally used for carving. He put a little more pressure on the knife. Suddenly, it slipped. The knife sliced off the round top of the stick that was to be the doll's head. George picked it up and sighed as he rolled the ball in his fingers.

"Hmm," mumbled George as he studied the ball. "This looks about the same size as my bullets. I wonder…."

George decided to load his gun with the wooden bullet. He rolled over on his stomach and studied the woods behind him. After awhile he saw a small animal moving through the brush. George aimed carefully. He pulled the trigger.

He let out a cheer as he saw the animal fall over. George ran into the woods. He let out a sigh of relief as he picked up the animal by its long ears. The rabbit would make a fine meal for a starving man. *Patches should appreciate it too*, thought George. Roasted rabbit replaced horse on the menu.

The meal did much to improve George's spirits. He also began to think a bit clearer. Being a part of the expedition was a great honor and a great adventure. Still, he had to be realistic. He had chased the group for two weeks.

He began to realize that he may never catch up. He may never find them. In fact, there was a good possibility that he could get even more lost. It was a big, unexplored country. George decided that it was time to go home.

There were French trappers and traders who moved up and down the river. He knew if he headed back down the river, he would eventually find someone who could help him. It was a sad decision, but a necessary one, reasoned George. He knew he was fortunate his wooden bullet didn't fracture into pieces. He may never be able to kill another animal with a piece of wood.

He knew the decision also gave him another option. If he couldn't take the horse back to Captain Lewis anyway, Patches would be available if George found himself near starvation. It was a last resort, and he hoped he didn't have to do that. He liked horses and didn't want to have to harm them.

George had proven that with Frisky. It would not be unusual for a lame horse to be shot. He would have been better off to have all that meat from the horse. He had learned to dry it from the Indians. It would have been enough to live off of for quite awhile.

He didn't regret not shooting Frisky. He hoped the horse was healing up somewhere. Maybe he would even see Frisky again as he moved back down the river. Feeling satisfied for the first time in weeks, George slept peacefully that night.

It was the sound of grazing that woke George up the next morning. He couldn't believe Patches could be that hungry as he tried to wake up. He opened one eye. He saw a large creature about thirty feet away. Patches looked a lot fatter and heavier than normal.

It was a foggy morning. That happened a lot by the river. As soon as the sun came up, that early morning fog would burn off. Then it felt quite steamy for awhile.

Just then, George felt something nudge his shoulder. He rolled over and stared into the nostrils of Patches the horse.

"How did you get over here that quickly?" asked George as he patted the horse on the nose.

Slowly George turned the other way. He let his eyes focus through the fog. He was filled with a little bit of fear as he recognized the animal. It was a buffalo. In fact, it was a herd of buffalo.

He was outnumbered greatly. Besides that, each animal was much bigger than him. Some of the buffalo had horns. It was possible they would leave him alone. Then again, if they perceived him to be a threat to their calves, they may go on the attack.

If he tried to shoot a buffalo with a wooden bullet, it just might roll over laughing at him. It would probably just bounce off its leathery hide. The bison could seem quite tame. They were not fearful of men. People could approach them.

Still, they were wild animals. They could turn in an instant and charge. They were extremely fast. They could run forty miles per hour for short distances. They could jump straight up in the air. They could even change direction almost instantly.

As George stared through the fog he began to realize there weren't just a few bison. There were hundreds. They were slowly making their way toward the river. George knew it was time to go. His journey down the river would have to begin now.

## Chapter 5
## Down the River

September 11, 1804

George rested on the river bank. He was exhausted and starving. Once again, Patches was starting to look like his only option for survival. He decided to climb on the back of the horse instead.

He hoped it would remind him how useful the horse was for travel. If his feet could vote, they would choose to keep the horse alive. Riding was just the break his tired and aching feet needed. He almost fell asleep while riding. His eyes drooped and his head dropped.

If he had been alert, he would have noticed a wonderful sight on the river. Instead, it was a voice calling out that caught his attention.

"Hello there!" said a man at the front of a boat.

George at first thought he was dreaming. He yawned and slowly opened his eyes. His jaw dropped at the sight. By now a canoe was rowing to shore. Captain Lewis was the first one to step ashore.

"We thought we'd never see you again, Shannon," grinned the captain.

"Same here, Captain," said George.

Captain Lewis looked at how frail George had become. He hadn't eaten anything but a few wild grapes and the one rabbit. His ammunition was gone.

"You look hungry enough to eat a horse," said the captain.

"I almost did," smiled George as he patted Patches.

"We were worried about you," said Captain Lewis.

"To be honest," said George, "I was worried about me too."

George Shannon had been lost for sixteen days. During that time he traveled about 240 miles alone. For days he had tried to catch up with the expedition. The problem was they were behind him the whole time.

"Don't ever get lost again," teased Captain Lewis as he patted George on the back. "That's an order!"

"Yes, sir!" smiled George.

That was an order George could not keep. Almost a year later on August 6, 1805 George once again found himself separated from the expedition. He once again followed a branch of a river thinking the others were ahead of him. It wasn't his fault this time. He was looking where the captain had said he was going to go. When the river became too difficult for boats to travel on, George figured out that the others had taken a different way.

After three days, he caught up. This time, he brought something back with him. He wasn't starved at all. In fact, he had managed to feed himself well. He had shot three deer and returned with their hides and some meat. The other men were the ones who were hungry this time. No one complained about George's hunting skills again.

George Shannon would later help prepare the first edition of the Lewis and Clark Journals in 1810. Later in life became a lawyer and a senator from Missouri. He lived from 1785 to 1836 and was buried in Palmyra, Missouri.

## William Clark's Journal Entries:

The following are journal entries from William Clark that tell about the day George Shannon was found. Many of the men on the expedition were asked to keep journals. Sometimes they wrote complete notes and added to them at later times. Historians think that may be the case with the two different accounts by William Clark. Dates were corrected in other versions of the story by comparing them to other journals.

Reading the entries, you may notice that William Clark was not the best speller. There are reasons for this. In 1806, a man named Noah Webster published a dictionary. It was his attempt to help develop standardized spelling for words used in America, taking into account some of the differences between how the language was spoken in England. He wanted to simplify words even more, but didn't quite succeed.

So William Clark was educated at a time when people used all different kinds of spellings for the same word. You can thank Noah Webster for creating the possibility of spelling bees and a way to write words that everyone agrees is the right way to spell them. Then again, if you don't do well on a spelling test, you might want to blame Noah Webster. If it weren't for him, you might just have gotten away with it. In the journal articles the misspelled words are in bold print. Can you spell the words correctly? If not, a Webster's dictionary would be a big help.

### Version 1

Septr. 11th Tuesday 1804 Set out early a Cloudy morning the river **verry** wide from one hill to the other, with many Sand bars passed the **Isd**. on which we lay at a mile passed three **Isds**. one on the L. S. (¼ of a mile from it on the L. S. a village of little Dogs. I Killed four, this village is 800 yards wide & 970 yds. long on a **jentle** Slope of a hill in a plain, those animals are **noumerous**) the other two Islands are on the S. S. the river is **verry** Shallow & wide, the [boat?] got a ground Several times- The man G

Shannon, who left us with the horses above the Mahar Village, and **beleving** us to be a head pushed on as long as he Could, joined us he Shot away what **fiew** Bullets he had with him, and in a **plentifull Countrey** like to have **Starvd**. he was 12 days without provision, Subsisting on Grapes at the Same the **Buffalow**, would Come within 30 yards of his Camp, one of his horses gave out & he left him before his last **belluts** were Consumed- I saw 3 large **Spoted** foxes **to day** a black tailed Deer, & Killed a Buck elk & 2 Deer, one **othr** Elk 2 Deer & a **Porkipine** Killed to day at 12 **oclock** it became Cloudy and rained all the afternoon, & night.

## Version 2

Septr. 11th Tuesday 1804

here the man who left us with the horses 22 days ago and has been **a head** ever Since joined, us nearly Starved to Death, he had been 12 days without any thing to **eate** but Grapes & one **Rabit**, which he Killed by shooting a piece of hard Stick in place of a ball. This man **Supposeing** the boat to be **a head** pushed on as long as he Could, when he became weak and **fiable deturmined** to lay by and **waite** for a **tradeing** boat, which is expected Keeping one horse for the last **resorse**,- thus a man had like to have Starved to death in a land of Plenty for the want of **Bulletes** or Something to kill his meat we Camped on the L. S. above the mouth of a run a hard rain all the **after noon**, & most of the night, with hard wind from the N W. I walked on Shore the fore part of this day over Some broken Country which **Continus** about 3 miles back & then is **leavel** & rich all Plains, I saw Several foxes & Killed a Elk & 2 Deer. & **Squirels** the men with me killed an Elk, 2 Deer & a Pelican.

# Abraham Lincoln

Stories by Brian Davis
Illustrations by Ron Wheeler



## Abe and Kiwami



## Vocabulary Words

bartering
biography
determination
discreetly
intently
partridge
persistence
persuasive
precarious
preoccupied

### Non-Fiction

*Non-fiction can take different forms. Following is a type of non-fiction called a biography. Bio means life and graph means to write. So the word biography means to tell the story about a person's life. Sometimes it is about a whole person's life, or it can be about a specific event in a person's life.*

*Today you'll read a story about an event in a boy's life that occurred when he was only ten years old. Austin Gallaher lived from 1806 to 1898. He lived in Kentucky and grew up in a pioneer family.*

## Pioneer Boys

Growing up in a pioneer family could be lonely at times. Austin's closest friend lived two miles away. One day, his mother woke him up early. His mother asked him if he would like to go with her. She was going to his friend's house. She wanted to visit Nancy, his friend's mother.

Austin was very excited to go. He quickly rose from bed and dressed. He was ready for the long walk. Austin enjoyed walking through the woods. He planned out the day as they walked along the narrow path. The summer sunlight broke through the trees.

Austin thought of the last summer. He enjoyed playing with his friend at school. It was too cold to attend school in the winter. School was in session only during the summer months. Not enough scholars (students) were available this year. That meant that Austin didn't get to see friends very often.

He thought of the first day of school the previous year. His friend's sister wanted her brother to play with the girls. Not all of the scholars at the school were children. Some of the big boys were full grown men. She was very protective and watched over him like a mother. Sometimes when the road was muddy, she even carried her little brother to school.

Austin knew his friend could take care of himself. The seven-year-old boy was three years younger than Austin. You couldn't tell by looking. They were about the same size.

His friend was also very strong. Austin remembered that as they neared a small cabin in the woods. He heard a familiar chopping sound. It was his friend swinging an axe and chopping wood.

The young boy looked up as Austin and his mother entered the clearing. He dropped the axe and came running. The barefoot boy wore homemade clothes. The trousers rose several inches above his ankles. The boy seemed to have grown since Austin last saw him.

Soon Austin and his friend were off exploring in the woods. The boys didn't have bikes, baseballs or basketball hoops. Their toys were the rocks, streams, and animals of the forest. Even the trees were turned into toys. The boys bent saplings over. They rode the young trees like horses.

Next, they tossed rocks into a little stream called Knob Creek. They made little boats with sticks and leaves. The current carried the boats away. They followed along the bank of the creek. It was difficult. The water was moving more swiftly than normal because of recent rains.

Austin's friend knew this part of the creek well. He had spent many hours in the woods. He would often go hunting with his father or mother. Both were very good with a rifle. Austin's friend knew the best places to find berries. Austin was grateful because he was ready for a snack.

Next, the young boy pointed to the other side, "Right up there we saw a covey of partridges yesterday. Let's go over and get some of them."

There was only one problem. The stream was swollen. It was too wide to jump across. The boys walked along the bank. They came to a log that had fallen across the creek. The water rushed a few feet below the log. It looked simple enough to cross.

They looked over the narrow log. "Let's coon it," said the younger boy. Austin was a little worried for his friend. He decided to go first to make sure it was safe. He got down on his hands and knees. He scooted across like a raccoon. Soon he was on the other side.

Austin took a big sigh of relief. The other boy carefully crawled onto the log. He got to the center before looking down. Suddenly the young boy began to tremble. The water seemed so powerful. He was suspended only a few feet above it.

"Don't look down, nor up, nor sideways. Look right at me and hold on tight!" said Austin as he began to make his way to his friend.

It was too late. With a great splash the young boy fell. He landed in eight feet of rushing water. Austin knew he would be in just as bad shape if he jumped in after him. Neither boy was a very good swimmer.

Austin raced along the shore. He grabbed a stick. He held it out to the floating boy. The young boy grasped it with both hands. He held on tightly as Austin pulled him to shore. Grabbing him by the arms, Austin pulled him to shore.

The young boy seemed almost dead. Austin shook him and then rolled him on the ground. Water poured from the young boy's mouth. The boy coughed and choked, but was soon back to normal.

The friend looked at Austin, "Promise me that you won't tell anyone about this as long as I live."

Their mothers were very strict with them. Austin agreed. If their parents found out they would have even fewer opportunities to play together. The rest of the afternoon was spent away from the creek.

Austin kept his promise until his friend died from an assassin's bullet many years later. Little did Austin know that he changed history that day. He saved a young boy that would one day be famous. Austin's friend would grow up to be the sixteenth president of the United States. The young boy that he pulled from the flooded stream was named Abraham Lincoln.

*****

Pioneer Boys was written from details of an interview with Austin Gallaher. Additional details were added from an interview with Susan Riney Yeager, the daughter of Abraham Lincoln's first school teacher. She attended the school session with him and remembered him well. She didn't realize the Abe that she knew as a boy was the same Abraham Lincoln that became president until after his death. In his boyhood years, Abraham and his family pronounced their last name as Linkhorn.

*****

*Another form of non-fiction is a newspaper article. Newspaper articles are short and have a very narrow focus. They have a single topic. Generally, newspaper articles answer the questions who, what, where, when, and why. Suppose in 1816 someone had written a newspaper article about Abraham's near drowning. It might have read something like this:*

A frightening mishap nearly cost a young boy his life yesterday. Austin Gallaher, age 10 and Abraham Lincoln, age 7, both of Knob Creek were playing in the woods on the Lincoln homestead. The two boys decided to cross rain swollen Knob Creek to investigate a covey of partridges.

As it was too far to jump, the boys decided to crawl across a log. Austin made it safely and Abraham proceeded to follow. Midway across the log, young Abraham froze with fear. Losing his balance, the frightened boy plunged into the creek.

Neither boy being a powerful swimmer, Abe found himself in a precarious situation. Thinking quickly, Austin rescued the boy with a stick. Austin pulled the nearly dead boy ashore. After coughing up some water, Abe was soon back to normal. When asked what he thought of his rescuer, young Abe replied, "If Austin Gallaher ever runs for president, I'm voting for him."

*Sometimes the main purpose of non-fiction is to present information for research. An encyclopedia is a collection of books that have alphabetized articles over a great variety of things, people, events, and much more. If you wanted to find out more about Abraham Lincoln's childhood, you would find the book that had articles that begin with the letter L, since people are alphabetized by their last names.*

*For someone as well known as Abraham Lincoln, an encyclopedia article may have information about all periods of his life. People who are less known may only have information about specific events that they were involved with. An encyclopedia article about the early part of Abraham Lincoln's life might look like this:*

## Abraham Lincoln, the Early Years

Abraham Lincoln was born February 12, 1809 near Elizabethtown Kentucky. His father was Thomas Lincoln. Abraham's father was married to Nancy Hanks. Their first child was a girl named Sarah. She was born two years before her brother.

Like many families on the frontier, the Lincolns had little money. They bought a farm on credit and met most of their needs by living off the land. Both Thomas and Sarah were good with the rifle and able to hunt for much of their food.

At the age of 4, Abraham moved with his family to a larger and better farm near a stream called Knob Creek. The family lived there until Abraham was the age of 7. It was at Knob Creek that Abraham first attended school. His earliest teacher was Zachariah Riney. Abraham was a good student and was very successful in school. But most of his education happened in the home. His mother could read and write. She even managed to teach Thomas how to write his name.

In 1816, Thomas Lincoln decided to move his family after a dispute arose over the ownership of his farm. He built a small boat and headed downstream to a place called Thompson's Ferry. Abe's father traveled inland and found a place to build a cabin near what became Gentryville, Indiana.

At the age of seven, Abraham learned to use an ax to help clear the land for farming. Their only shelter for the first year was a three walled cabin. The fourth side was left open. A fire was built at the opening. This eliminated a need for a proper chimney.

In the autumn of the following year a sickness broke out among the settlers in the area. There were no doctors within thirty miles. Many people died. Abraham's mother, Nancy, was among those who fell ill and died.

The Lincoln family was very sad. Abraham felt saddened by the loss for the rest of his life. The next year, Thomas Lincoln married another woman. Her name was Sarah Bush Johnston. She was a young widow with three children of her own.

Sarah was very fond of Abraham. She encouraged him to learn as much as he could. Abraham learned to read and write although he had less than one year's worth of schooling spread out over nine years. Abraham loved to read, even though books were scarce. After reading a book, Abraham didn't need to read it a second time. His sharp mind was able to remember it.

It was good thing because Abraham actually had very little time to learn. He worked very hard on the family farm. He also hired himself out to others in need of help farming a field, clearing a forest, or building split rail fences. His determination to learn, despite many obstacles taught him not only the value of education, but also the value of persistence. The ability to learn and persist would become important characteristics of Abraham Lincoln that would ultimately lead to the Presidency.

*Another kind of non-fiction is a persuasive essay. The author of a persuasive essay is writing to get you to agree with his or her point of view. The goal of the author is to lead the reader to form an opinion based on an idea. Facts are presented as well as the author's opinions or interpretation of the facts. The author should target ideas based on who they hope to convince. Read the persuasive essay about Abraham Lincoln.*

## Abraham Lincoln the Greatest President

Abraham Lincoln was the greatest president in the history of the United States. Abraham came from a humble background and is a great example of how anyone can achieve in this country. He had very little formal education, but managed to learn to read, write, and do arithmetic with very little help. Abraham taught himself to be a lawyer because he wanted to help people. He ran for public office several times and started businesses. Very often he failed, but he never gave up.

He was also a great leader who led the country through one of its most painful time periods. When the Confederate States left the Union in the Civil War, Abraham Lincoln did not back down. He felt as president it was his responsibility to keep all the states together. He understood the importance of unity in building a strong nation.

He was also a very forgiving man. While some wanted to punish the people in the states that left the Union, Abraham Lincoln wanted to forgive them. He wanted to restore order and make all the states work together again. There is great wisdom in being forgiving. Abraham Lincoln was only interested in healing a nation that had been torn apart by war.

Abraham Lincoln disliked slavery. On January 1, 1863 he issued the Emancipation Proclamation. As president, he declared that the slaves in the rebelling states were now free. This led to the Thirteenth Amendment to the United States Constitution. The amendment made all slavery illegal in the United States.

Although we most often think of Abraham Lincoln's presidency in connection with the civil war, he also did other great things. On May 20, 1862 he approved the Federal Homestead Law. This gave families 160 acres of land if they worked on it for five years in the new territories in the United States. Many farmers were given the opportunity to own their own land in the western frontier. Do you like turkey dinners in November? On October 3, 1863, Abraham Lincoln made Thanksgiving a national holiday to be celebrated on the last Thursday of every November.

Abraham Lincoln's life story is a great inspiration. He showed great wisdom in standing up for the Union. The president showed great mercy in forgiving the Confederate States. He showed great compassion by freeing the slaves. Abraham Lincoln showed great vision for encouraging the settlement in the west. He gave us many reasons for thanksgiving. Abraham Lincoln should be recognized as the greatest president in the history of the United States of America.

*The opposite of non-fiction is fiction. There are different kinds of fiction. Historical fiction is a story that is not true, but involves people or events found in history. There are details or parts of the story that are true, but much of the story is made up.*

## Abe and Kiwami

### Chapter 1
### Indian Attack

"Hoo, hoo!"

Sarah turned around, not expecting to see an owl. She was right. Sitting up in a tree was her neighbor Jim. They were both nine years old.

"What are you doing up there hooting, Jim?" asked Sarah.

"Hiding," answered Tom, "from Indians. Get up here. Quick!"

"Jim, Indians can climb trees. Besides, Abe's out here somewhere. Ma sent me to fetch him. Can you see him from up there?"

"No," said Jim.

"Well, are you going to stay up there all day or come down and help me find Abe?" asked Sarah.

"I can help," sighed Jim, "But I plan on keeping my scalp. First sign of Indians and you can find me up the nearest tree."

"No one has seen an Indian in these parts in over two years," Sarah reassured him.

"The way I figure it," explained Jim "the Indians are way overdue, and I do know someone who's seen an Indian around here."

"Who," asked Sarah? She was very doubtful.

"Me, today!" said Jim. "You think I'd hide in a tree just from fear of an Indian?"

"You saw an Indian?" asked Sarah.

"Nearly killed by one as a matter of fact," Jim lifted the hair on his forehead. There was a small scratch. It was fresh but didn't look deadly.

"Don't tell me," said Sarah. "They tried to scalp you and your head was too hard."

Jim stuck his lip out, "No, it was an arrow. It bounced off."

"Bounced off?" laughed Sarah.

"It's a miracle I survived," said Jim. "You should be glad I did too! You should be filled with gratitude that I'm alive to warn you."

"So what did this Indian look like?" asked Sarah.

Jim thought for a minute. He looked puzzled. "I guess I didn't actually see the Indian. I just saw the arrow."

"Can I see the arrow?" asked Sarah.

Jim frowned. "After I got hit, I took off running."

"Are you sure it wasn't just a stick falling from a tree? I was once almost hit by a falling tree limb."

"Do sticks have feathers? Do they fly sideways when they fall off trees? Do sticks half-kill boys?" asked Jim.

"They can scratch boys," smiled Sarah.

Jim started to get angry. Suddenly he stopped and turned his head slowly. He was listening intently. Jim put a finger to his lips to motion for Sarah to stay silent.

The wind rustled the leaves on the trees. Another sound was carried on the wind. Sarah heard it this time. It was voices, strange voices in a strange language.

The two children looked for a place to hide. A massive moss-covered log was just off the path. Sarah and Jim hid themselves. The voices were growing louder. Several people were coming their way.

Several men were walking through the woods. They were strange-looking men, dark skinned and very large. Neither Sarah nor Jim had ever seen men like these before. They wore brightly colored costumes. Dark lines were painted on their faces.

"Indians," whispered Jim.

Sarah nodded yes. She was sorry she hadn't taken Jim more seriously. Peeking over the log, she saw the men looking for something on the ground. They were carrying sticks and swatting at the underbrush. Maybe being up in a tree wouldn't have been such a bad idea.

Jim and Sarah quietly dug under the leaves. They were completely hidden by the time the men passed them by. Jim and Sarah could hear their voices speaking in the strange language. They held their breath when one of the Indians paused just a few feet away. He yelled out to someone behind him.

The other person yelled back. The voice surprised Sarah and Jim. The second voice wasn't the voice of a man. It was the voice of a young boy.

Sarah imagined that the man was the boy's father. It seemed as though he was telling the boy to keep up with the group. The shuffling sound of leaves let Sarah and Jim know that the man had walked off.

Soon, more footsteps approached. This time there were fewer. It was easy to tell the straggling young boy was coming. He answered when the man in the distance yelled to him again. Yet, there were two sets of footsteps.

Sarah heard something very familiar. It was a song, a song her mother had taught her. A young boy was singing the song. The boy's voice was also familiar. Sarah carefully pulled back the leaves.

She saw a barefoot and a raggedy trouser leg. The song was being sung by her brother. He always sang it when he was nervous. It calmed him down. Sarah nearly leaped out of the pile of leaves.

Jim held her back. He pointed to the Indian boy that was following Abe. The Indian was carrying a spear. It was obvious that Abe had been taken captive by Indians.

Sarah and Jim waited as the boys passed. They listened as the sound of crunching leaves faded into the distance. Only then did they quietly shed themselves of their leafy disguise. Sarah started to follow.

"What are you doing?" whispered Jim.

"They have Abe. We've got to follow them."

Jim hadn't seen Abe. He had kept his eyes closed the whole time he was buried under the leaves. He kept wishing he were up a tree rather than behind a log.

"Shouldn't we go get help?" answered Jim.

"Yes, we should," answered Sarah, "but we need to find the Indian camp. Then we'll know where to bring the help. We have no choice but to follow."

"Okay," sighed Jim, "but, if we get scalped our folks are sure to give us a good whippin'."

## Chapter 2
## Captive Abe

Sarah and Jim stayed on the trail of Abe and the Indians. They had to stay far back to prevent being spotted. Still, it wasn't difficult to track them. Sarah and Jim simply followed the trail of freshly disturbed leaves.

The path led to a spot on Knob Creek. It was near a rocky outcrop. Abe and Sarah often played there. They pretended it was a cave. It was something like a cave. The rocky ledge provided a handy place to wait out a storm.

The Indians must have been using it for shelter. Sarah and Jim hid in the brush and spied on them. The Indians had built a very small campfire. Two women were plucking a freshly killed turkey. A few minutes later, three men and two small boys joined them. One of the boys was Abe.

Sarah kept a close eye on her brother. He seemed to be ok. Actually, he didn't even seem that afraid. Sarah wondered if her brother understood what kind of danger he was in. The adult Indians didn't seem to be paying much attention to Abe. He could have easily slipped away unnoticed except for the boy that was watching him.

Sarah waved to Abe, trying to get his attention. He didn't notice her. She crept closer, all the time discreetly waving. Jim watched from a distance. He wanted to help, but didn't want to get caught. He might be their only hope for getting help.

"Don't worry," whispered Jim to Sarah, "I'm ready to run for help at any time."

"Knowing you're ready to run away is so comforting," she whispered back.

Abe was too busy playing with the other boy to notice his sister. Suddenly one of the men looked up and saw her. Jim quickly planned his escape route, but then the actions of the Indians puzzled him.

Instead of running to Sarah, the Indians started running away. They paid no attention to Abe. Jim also noticed something else for the first time. There were bands of iron around the ankles of the Indians. Between the bands were short metal chains that made it difficult for the Indians to run.

Abe quickly chased them down. He was talking and pointing. "She's my sister. Don't be afraid."

Although they spoke a different language, the Indians somehow got the message. Maybe they just didn't want to run away from all the food they had gathered. The Indians looked very hungry. They all stopped and smiled and nodded.

Jim had never met real Indians before. He stepped out of the bushes. Again the Indians jumped back. Jim had never met anyone who was afraid of him before. It was a strange feeling of power.

“Greetings, Indians,” waved Jim. “I come in peace.”

“They’re not Indians,” corrected Sarah. “They’re slaves, escaped slaves would be my guess.”

“Then why are they dressed like Indians?” asked Jim.

One of the slaves stepped forward. The man was easily of the oldest of the group. He walked over to Jim and lifted up the hair on the boy’s forehead. Jim began to shake.

“Oh no! He’s going to scalp me!”

The man pulled his hand back and laughed. “I’m not going to hurt you, boy. I just wanted to see if you’re the one we’ve been looking for.”

“Am I?” Jim was almost too afraid to ask.

“Were you shot with an arrow today?” asked the man.

Jim nodded, “You’re…you’re not going to finish the job are you?”

The man shook his head no. “No one meant to hurt you. Little Kiwami was shooting at a rabbit,” the man explained as he pointed to the young boy standing next to Abe. “The arrow went astray. He ran back here to get us. We didn’t even know Abe and Kiwami had snuck off. Next thing we know, Abe’s telling me they shot his friend Jim. That’s when we started looking for you.”

“See, I was telling the truth,” Jim said to Sarah. Then he looked over the group, “but why are you dressed as Indians and why the funny language? You speak English all right, better than I do I suppose.”

“We are from Africa,” the man explained.

“Is that near Boston?” asked Jim.

The man smiled, “Africa is far away. We had to cross an ocean on a ship. I came nearly twenty years ago. My friends arrived just a few months ago. I learned English over the years. They speak different languages in Africa. Different tribes have different languages.”

“Tribes! So that’s why you’re dressed as Indians!” exclaimed Jim.

“We’re dressed as Indians because these are the only clothes we have,” the man explained. “We didn’t have these until a few days ago. We were traveling through the woods at night. That’s the safest time for us to move about. Plus, we have the stars to guide us.”

“We saw a small group of Indians camped near a stream. I didn’t want to stir them up, so we kept our distance. As we walked through the woods we came upon a pack of wolves. They were somewhat preoccupied with something in a large tree. We turned to go the other way, but a voice cried out.”

“We each grabbed a stick and chased the wolves away. Next thing we knew, an Indian jumped to the ground. He couldn’t have been any older than you. The boy wasn’t in the best of condition. I’d say the wolves got to him before he got to the tree.”

"Having already passed the camp, we had a pretty good idea where he belonged. We couldn't just leave him. The wolves would come back. So I picked him up and carried him to the Indian camp."

"It turns out the boy was the son of a chief. He was most grateful. The chief saw the pitiful state of our clothing and gladly gave us what we now wear, as well as a few bows and arrows."

Sarah apologized to Jim, "I'm sorry I didn't believe you. I can see why you thought you were shot by Indians. I guess you're not so crazy after all."

"I accept your apology," replied Jim, "but next time I get half-killed you better believe me."

"Every time you get half-killed in the future, I will believe you," promised Sarah.

## Chapter 3
## A Plan for Freedom

The door squeaked louder than Jim had expected. It normally didn't matter how loud a hinge squeaked on the farm. Normally, he wasn't trying to sneak six slaves dressed as Indians into the shed. That's why they waited until dark to sneak around.

The slaves would be much better off without their chains. Jim's father was a farrier. He made and put horseshoes on horses. Jim's father had all kinds of blacksmithing tools. The old slave knew just how to use them.

"Who's there?" shouted a voice in the darkness. It came from the direction of a small cabin several yards away. A lantern glowed in the darkness.

"It's me, Mom," shouted Jim. "I'm going to practice hammering."

"Practice hammering?"

"So I can help Pa when he gets back," explained Jim. "I'm going to build up strong muscles."

"Be careful," yelled Jim's mother.

"What's all the yelling about?" said a voice behind Jim.

He jumped and spun around. Sarah and Abe were right behind him. He hadn't seen them coming in the dark. He had given up on them when they didn't meet him at the creek.

"Where have you been?"

"We couldn't get away," said Sarah. "Some strangers came down the road. They had a wagon with two dogs in a box. They're tracking dogs named Buck and Jo. The men are going to use them in the morning to track the runaway slaves."

"They asked my dad to help," said Abe, "Even said they'd pay him."

"What did he say?" asked Jim.

"I don't know that slavery is wrong, but it doesn't seem right," smiled Abe. "That's what he said."

Sarah added, "He said he wouldn't try to help'em, and he wouldn't try to stop'em."

"Good," said Jim. "Your pa knows the backwoods too well."

"That's why we followed them," said Sarah. "I offered to help them."

"You what?" Jim's jaw dropped open.

"We have a plan," smiled Abe.

"It was all Abe's idea," said Sarah

"Jim, Jim," whispered a voice from inside the shed.

Jim had forgotten all about the reason the slaves had come to his farm.

"Is it safe to hammer now?" asked the old slave. "Can we make some noise?"

The children went into the shed. They watched as the old slave skillfully cut off the bands from the feet of the slaves. Kiwami was the first to be freed. Abe handed the young boy some old clothes. He explained his plan to the old slave, who in turn translated it to the other slaves. They seemed to like the idea.

Abe and Sarah headed back toward Knob Creek. They didn't want to stay out in the woods too late at night. It was still full of wild animals. They just needed to get things set up for the next morning.

A frost was on the ground when Sarah woke Abe up early in the morning. The sun was just coming over the horizon. Sarah found the slave hunters and the dogs in a camp near the meeting house.

There were two men with the dogs. They were professional slave hunters. The men were very rough looking. They had rotted teeth and scraggly beards. Their clothes were dirty. They had obviously not had a bath in quite awhile.

The men offered Sarah dried biscuits, deer jerky, and hot coffee in a dirty cup. She crinkled her nose, and then remembered to be polite.

"No, thank you. I've already eaten."

"So you think you saw the slaves in the woods?" asked one of the men.

"Yes, sir," said Sarah. "There were three men, two women, and a little boy. Six slaves altogether. They had these funny looking bracelets around their ankles and chains between their feet. The strangest part is that they were dressed like Indians."

The man smiled. He pulled a silver coin out of his pocket. The man took Sarah's hand, placed the coin in it, and closed her fingers around it tightly.

"That's yours to keep, little lady," said the man. "All you have to do is show us the place where you saw the slaves. We just need a starting point. Old Buck and Jo will take it from there."

The other man had finished eating. He walked to a tree where Old Buck and Jo were tied. The man fed the dogs a few scraps.

Sarah opened the palm of her hand. She stared at the coin. Her family rarely had real money. They got most of what they needed by bartering. She couldn't help but smile as she looked at the coin. There was genuine excitement in her voice. She only hoped she'd get to keep the coin after Abe's plan unfolded.

“I know where it is! I know right where it is! They were camped down by the creek.”

Sarah led the men down to Knob Creek. “Look,” Sarah pointed to a jagged rock. A piece of buckskin was on the rock. “This looks like part of their Indian disguise.”

The men had Old Buck and Jo sniffed the cloth. The dogs quickly picked out a trail. They began howling and pulling on the ropes tied around their collars. The men took off into the woods. Sarah followed at a distance. Her job was done, but she wanted to make sure all went as planned.

“Hoo, hoo,” came a sound from a tree.

Sarah looked up. Jim and Abe sat on a limb. Sarah climbed up to meet them. From the top of a tree, they could look down a meadow in a small valley.

“It looks like they’re heading in the right direction,” smiled Sarah.

“Which is the wrong direction,” giggled Abe.

“Making a scent trail with Kiwami’s clothes was a great idea Abe,” said Sarah.

“Those slave hunters will sure be surprised when they meet up with the real Indian tribe,” laughed Jim.

Far away in the opposite direction of the slave hunters, Kiwami and his family had escaped. After being freed from the chains, the runaways were able to move much quicker. They had not returned to their camp the night before, instead they followed Jim’s directions to a cave far away. Resting from a hard night’s journey, young Kiwami thought of his friend Abe. Somehow, Kiwami believed they would not be the last slaves Abraham Lincoln would help free.

# Rip Van Winkle

Original Story by Washington Irving

Adapted by Brian Davis
Illustrations by Ron Wheeler



***Rip Van Winkle*** *first appeared in Washington Irving's collection of stories, The Sketch Book of Geoffrey Crayon, Gent., published in 1819.*

A WRITING OF DIEDRICH KNICKERBOCKER.

The following Tale was found among the papers of the late Diedrich Knickerbocker, an old gentleman of New York. He was very curious in the Dutch history of the province, and the stories of the **descendants** from its **primitive** settlers. His historical studies, however, did not lie as much among books as among men. He found the old men of the villages, and still more their wives, to be rich in legendary stories, so invaluable to true history. Whenever, therefore, he happened upon a genuine Dutch family, snugly shut up in its low-roofed farm-house, he looked upon it as a little valuable book, and studied it with great enthusiasm.

WASHINGTON IRVING 1819

## Chapter 1

WHOEVER has made a voyage up the Hudson River must remember the Catskill Mountains. They are a part of the great Appalachian chain. They are seen to the west of the river. Swelling up to great heights, they watch over the surrounding country.

Every change of season, weather, or even hour of the day, produces a change in the colors and shapes of these mountains. They are regarded by all good wives as perfect **barometers**.

When the weather is fair and settled, they are clothed in blue and purple. The mountains make clear outlines on the evening sky. At other times, they will gather clouds about their summits. The last rays of the setting sun glow like a crown of glory.

At the foot of these mountains, a traveler may have seen the light smoke curling up from a village. The shingle-roofs gleam among the trees. It is a little village, of great antiquity. It had been founded by some of the **Dutch** colonists, in the early times of the province. There were some of the houses of the original settlers. They were built of small yellow bricks brought from Holland. They had **latticed** windows and **gable** fronts, with **weathervanes** swinging on the roof tops.

In one of these very houses a simple good-natured fellow lived. The home was sadly worn-down and weather-beaten. This simple good-natured man was named Rip Van Winkle. His story begins at the time the country was still a province of Great Britain.

Rip Van Winkle was a kind neighbor. Moreover, he was a **hen-pecked** husband. Indeed, being a hen-pecked husband led to the **meekness** of spirit which made him so popular. His kind temper was formed in the fiery furnace of the trouble his wife caused him. If an angry wife could be considered a hidden blessing, Rip Van Winkle was, indeed, very blessed.

He was a great favorite among all the wives of the village. They took his side in all family **squabbles**. Whenever they talked about those matters, the blame was laid on **Dame** Van Winkle.

The children of the village loved Rip too. They would shout with joy whenever Rip Van Winkle approached. He assisted at their sports and made their toys. He taught them to fly kites and shoot marbles. He told exciting stories.

The children surrounded him as he walked through the village. They clung to his arms. They climbed on his back. They played a thousand tricks on him. Rip took it all in with a smile. Not even a dog would bark at him throughout the neighborhood.

The great problem in Rip's character was avoidance to all kinds of profitable labor. It was not from the lack of trying or laziness. He would sit on a wet rock, with a fishing rod all day without a murmur. He was patient even when he never got a single nibble.

He would carry a gun on his shoulder for hours. He trudged through woods and swamps. He climbed up hill and down into the ditches just to shoot a few squirrels or wild pigeons. He would never refuse to help a neighbor even with the hardest work. He was the best at husking corn or building stone-fences.

The women of the village too, used to ask him to run their errands. He did the little odd jobs that their less helpful husbands would not do for them. In a word, Rip was ready to help anybody but his own family.

He did little work on his own farm. In fact, he declared it was of no use to work on his farm. It was the worst piece of ground in the whole country. Everything about it went wrong. His fences were always falling to pieces. His cows would either go astray, or graze in the garden. Weeds were sure to grow quicker in his fields than anywhere else. Each time he started to plow the fields, it began to rain.

Over time, the family farm had dwindled away under his care. He sold it away, acre by acre. There was little more left than a mere patch of Indian corn and potatoes. It was the worst farm in the neighborhood.

His children too, were as ragged and wild as if they belonged to nobody. His son Rip was a child born in his own likeness. He inherited the **neglectful** habits along with the old clothes of his father. Young Rip followed at his mother's heels, wearing his father's cast-off clothes.

Rip Van Winkle, however, was one of those happy people. He would always choose the easiest way, like eating white bread or brown. His choice was whichever could be had with the least thought or trouble. He would rather starve on a penny than work for a dollar.

If left to himself, he would have whistled life away in perfect peace. His wife continually yelled in his ears about his **idleness**, his carelessness, and the ruin he was bringing on his family. Morning, noon, and night, her tongue never ceased going. Everything he said or did was sure to produce a shower of **criticism**.

Rip had but one way of replying to all lectures. He shrugged his shoulders, shook his head and cast up his eyes. He said nothing. This, however, always **provoked** a fresh **tirade** from his wife. He felt he had little choice but to take to the outside of the house. That is the only side which belongs to a hen-pecked husband.

## Chapter 2

Rip's sole comfort in his family was his dog, Wolf. The dog was as much hen-pecked as his master. Dame Van Winkle regarded them as companions in laziness. She even looked upon Wolf as the cause of his master's going so often astray.

Still, Wolf was an honorable dog. He was as courageous an animal as ever **scoured** the woods. That courage couldn't withstand the never ending terrors of his master's wife.

The moment Wolf entered the house his tail drooped to the ground or curled between his legs. He sneaked about with a feeling of **doom**. He kept a cautious watch on Dame Van Winkle. At the least threat of a broomstick or **ladle**, he would fly to the door with yelping **anticipation**.

Times grew worse and worse with Rip Van Winkle as years of marriage rolled on. A sour temper never sweetens with age. A sharp tongue is the only edged tool that grows sharper with constant use. For a long while he used to console himself. When driven from home, he met with his friends. They were the **sages**, philosophers, and other idle people of the village. The friends met on a bench beside a small **inn**. The sign showed a portrait of His Majesty George the Third.

Here they used to sit in the shade through a long, lazy summer's day. They talked over village gossip or told endless sleepy stories about nothing. Once in awhile, a newspaper fell into their hands from some passing traveler. That sparked **profound** discussions that would have interested the finest **statesman**.

How **solemnly** they would listen to the newspaper contents. The articles were read by Derrick Van Bummel, the schoolmaster. He easily read the most gigantic words in the dictionary.

The opinions of this group were completely controlled by Nicholas Vedder. He was the owner of the inn. Nicholas sat at the door from morning until night. He moving just enough to avoid the sun and keep in the shade of a large tree. The neighbors could tell the hour by his movements as accurately as by a clock. It is true, he rarely spoke. He smoked his pipe constantly.

His followers, however perfectly understood him. They knew how to gather his opinions. When anything that was read or related displeased him, he was observed to smoke his pipe **vehemently**. He sent forth short, frequent, and angry puffs. When pleased, he would inhale the smoke slowly. The pipe made peaceful clouds. Sometimes he would slowly nod his head to show perfect approval.

Even with his friends Rip was not safe. Dame Van Winkle would find him. She yelled at the friends as well as Rip. She accused them of helping her husband be lazy.

Poor Rip was at last reduced almost to **despair**. The woods became his only escape from the labor of the farm and the **clamor** of his wife. Here he would sometimes seat himself at the foot of a tree. He shared the contents of his knapsack with Wolf.

Rip had sympathy for the dog. "Poor Wolf," he would say, "your mistress gives you a dog's life. Never mind, my lad. While I live you shall never lack a friend!" Wolf would wag his tail. The dog looked **wistfully** in his master's face. If dogs can feel pity I believe he felt the same way for Rip.

On a fine **autumnal** day, Rip found himself on one of the highest parts of the Catskill Mountains. He was hunting squirrels. The mountain walls echoed the shots from his gun.

It was late in the afternoon. Panting and fatigued, he threw himself on the grass. From an opening between the trees he could overlook all the lower country. He could see many a mile of rich woodland. He saw at a distance the Hudson River. It moved on its silent but **majestic** course. On the other side he looked down into a deep mountain **ravine**. The bottom was filled with sharp rocks that had fallen from cliffs. Darkness was falling in the low places.

For some time Rip lay enjoying the scenery. Evening was gradually advancing. The mountains began to throw their long blue shadows over the valleys. Rip saw that it would be dark long before he could reach the village. He heaved a heavy sigh when he thought about Dame Van Winkle. She was sure to be furious.

As he was about to descend, he heard a voice from a distance.

"Rip Van Winkle! Rip Van Winkle!"

He looked round. He could see nothing but a crow winging its lonely flight across the mountain. He thought he imagined the voice. Rip turned again to descend. He heard the same cry ring through the still evening air: "Rip Van Winkle! Rip Van Winkle!"

Wolf bristled up his back, giving a low growl. The dog cowered at his master's side. The dog looked fearfully into the ravine. Rip now felt fear coming over him. He looked anxiously in the same direction. Rip thought he saw a strange figure slowly climbing up the rocks. The person was bending under the weight of something he carried on his back. Rip was surprised to see any human being in this lonely place. Rip supposed it to be a neighbor in need of his help. He hurried down to give it.

As he neared, Rip was surprised by the stranger's appearance. He was a short, square-built old fellow. He had thick bushy hair, and a grizzled beard. His dress was of the antique Dutch fashion. He bore on his shoulder a stout keg. It seemed full of liquid. The stranger made signs for Rip to approach. The man wanted Rip to assist him with the load.

## Chapter 3

Though rather shy and distrustful, Rip complied with his usual willingness. They **clambered** up a narrow gully. It was apparently the dry bed of a mountain stream. As they climbed, Rip every now and then heard long rumblings. It sounded like distant thunder. The sound seemed to come out of a deep ravine.

He paused for an instant to listen. Rip supposed it to be the muttering of a thunder-shower. They often take place in the mountain heights. He proceeded. Passing through the ravine, they came to a hollow. It was like a small **amphitheater**. They were surrounded by tall rock walls. Through the tree tops, he only caught glimpses of the blue sky and the bright evening clouds.

During the whole time, the stranger was silent. Rip wondered about the purpose for carrying the keg. There was something strange about the situation.

On entering the amphitheater, new objects of wonder presented themselves. On a level spot in the center was a company of odd-looking men playing at **ninepins**. They were dressed in an old **outlandish** fashion. Some had long knives in their belts. Most of them wore pants with very wide legs.

Their faces too, were **peculiar**. One had a large head, broad face, and small piggish eyes. The face of another seemed to consist entirely of nose. A white hat with a red feather covered the rest of the face. They all had beards. They were of various shapes and colors. There was one who seemed to be the **commander**.

He was a stout old gentleman. He had a weather-beaten **countenance** like a sailor. He wore a high-crowned hat and feather, red stockings, and high-heeled shoes, with roses in them. The whole group reminded Rip of the figures in an old painting. It hung in the parlor of the village pastor. It had been brought over from Holland at the time of the settlement.

What seemed particularly odd to Rip were the expressions on their faces. They were trying to have a good time, yet they had the saddest faces. There was a mysterious silence. Rip thought it was the saddest party he had ever seen. The only sound was the bowling balls. The rolling sound echoed along the mountains like rumbling peals of thunder.

As Rip and his companion approached them, they suddenly stopped playing. They stared at Rip with a statue-like gaze. His heart filled with fear. His knees knocked together. His companion now emptied the contents of the keg into large mugs. The man made signs to Rip to serve the others. He obeyed with fear and trembling. They drank the liquid in silence. When finished, they returned to their game.

In time Rip's awe and nervousness subsided. When no one was watching, he tasted the drink. He thought the flavor was excellent. He was naturally a thirsty soul. Soon, he was tempted to another mug full. One taste led to another. He drank so much that his eyes swam in his head. Rip fell into a deep sleep.

On waking, he found himself on the green grass where he had first seen the old man. He rubbed his eyes. It was a bright sunny morning. The birds were hopping and twittering among the bushes. The eagle was soaring overhead in the mountain breeze.

"Surely," thought Rip, "I have not slept here all night."

He remembered what had occurred before he fell asleep. The strange man with the keg-the mountain ravine-the area among the rocks-the games of ninepins-the mysterious drink.

"Oh! That drink! That wicked drink!" thought Rip. "What excuse shall I make to Dame Van Winkle?"

He looked around for his gun. In place of the clean, well-oiled gun, he found an old one lying by him. The barrel was rusted. The wooden stock was worm-eaten. He now suspected that the men of the mountain had played a trick on him. When he fell asleep, they robbed him of his gun. Wolf, too, had disappeared. The dog may have been hunting squirrel or partridge.

He whistled after him and shouted his name. The echoes repeated his whistle and shout, but no dog was to be seen. He decided to go back to the amphitheater. He would demand his dog and gun. As he rose to walk, he found himself stiff in the joints.

"These mountain beds do not agree with me," thought Rip, "and if I'm laid up at home, I shall have a terrible time with Dame Van Winkle."

With some difficulty he got down into the canyon. He found the gully up which he and his companion had climbed. To his astonishment a mountain stream was now foaming down it. It leaped from rock to rock. He scrambled up the bank. He worked his way through thickets of birch, **sassafras** with their egg-shaped leaves, and **witch-hazel**. Sometimes he was tripped up or entangled by the wild grape-vines.

Finally, he reached the opening through the cliffs to the amphitheater. It had changed overnight. No traces of such an opening remained. The rocks made a high wall. Over it poured a powerful waterfall.

## Chapter 4

Rip could travel no further. He again called and whistled after his dog. The only answer was the cawing of a flock of idle crows. They flew above a dry tree that overhung the ravine. The crows seemed to laugh at the poor man's problems.

What was to be done? The morning was passing away. Rip felt starving for his breakfast. He was sad to give up hunting for his dog and gun. He dreaded meeting up with his wife. Still, it would not do to starve among the mountains. He shook his head. Rip shouldered the rusty gun. With a heart full of trouble and anxiety, he turned his steps homeward.

As he approached the village, he met a number of people. He knew none of them. That surprised him. Rip thought he knew everyone in the surrounding country. Their dress, too, was of a different fashion from that to which he was **accustomed**. They all stared at him with equal looks of surprise.

Whenever they looked at him, they stroked their chins. The constant gesture made Rip to do the same. To his astonishment, he found his beard had grown a foot long!

He had now entered the skirts of the village. A troop of strange children ran at his heels. They made fun of him, and pointing at his gray beard.

The dogs, too, did not recognize him. They barked at him as he passed. The very village was **altered**. It was larger and more **populous**. There were rows of houses which he had never seen before. Familiar places had disappeared.

Strange names were over the doors. Strange faces were at the windows. Everything was strange. Rip began to think both he and the world around him were under a spell.

Surely this was his village. There stood the Catskill Mountains. There ran the silver Hudson River at a distance. There was every hill and valley precisely as it had always been.

Rip was very confused. "That drink last night," thought he, "has **addled** my poor head sadly!"

It was with some difficulty that he found the way to his own house. He approached with silent awe. Rip expected at every moment to hear the shrill voice of Dame Van Winkle. He found the house gone to decay. The roof had fallen in. The windows were shattered. The doors hung off the hinges. A half-starved dog that looked like Wolf was skulking about it. Rip called him by name. The mutt snarled, showed his teeth, and passed on.

"My very dog," sighed poor Rip, "has forgotten me!"

He entered the house. Dame Van Winkle had always kept it in neat order. It was empty and abandoned. He called loudly for his wife and children. The lonely rooms rang for a moment with his voice. The house fell silent.

He now hurried forth. He ran to his old resort, the village inn. It too was gone. A large rickety wooden building stood in its place. It had large open windows. Some of them were broken and mended with old hats and clothes. Over the door was painted, "The Union Hotel, by Jonathan Doolittle."

Instead of the great tree that used to shelter the quiet little Dutch inn, there now was a flag pole. From it was fluttering a strange flag. It was made up of stars and stripes.

He recognized the sign. However, the face of King George had changed. The red coat was changed for one of blue. A sword was held in the hand instead of a scepter. The head was decorated with a cocked hat, not a crown. Underneath was painted in large characters, GENERAL WASHINGTON.

There was, as usual, a crowd of folk about the door. Rip did not know any of them. The very character of the people seemed changed. There was a busy, bustling, tone about it. He was accustomed to a sleepy relaxed atmosphere.

He looked in vain for the wise Nicholas Vedder. His friend with the long pipe and puffs of tobacco smoke could not be found. He expected to see Van Bummel, the schoolmaster. He too was not around.

In place of these, a lean fellow, with his pockets full of handbills, was giving a speech about rights of citizens-elections-members of Congress-liberty-Bunker's hill-heroes of seventy-six-and other words, which were a perfect nonsense to the **bewildered** Rip Van Winkle.

Rip had a strange appearance. He had a long, grizzled beard. He carried the rusty gun. His clothes were unusual. An army of women and children followed at his heels. This quickly attracted the attention of the tavern politicians.

They crowded around him. The men eyed him from head to foot with great curiosity. The speaker bustled up to him. He drew Rip partly aside and asked, "On which side did you vote?"

Rip stared in total confusion. Another short but busy little fellow pulled him by the arm, "are you Federal or Democrat?" Rip was equally at a loss to comprehend the question.

A self-important old gentleman made his way through the crowd. He pushed the people aside to the right and left. The man planted himself before Rip Van Winkle. The man leaned on a cane. In a harsh tone he asked, "What brought you to the election with a gun on your shoulder? You have a mob at your heels! Do you mean to start a riot in the village?"

"My apologies gentlemen!" cried Rip, somewhat puzzled, "I am a poor quiet man. I was born in this place. I am a loyal subject of the king. May God bless him!"

Here a general shout burst from the bystanders. "A Tory! a Tory! A spy! A refugee! Grab him! Away with him!"

It was with great difficulty that the self-important man restored order. He demanded again of the unknown culprit, "What are you here for? Whom are you seeking?"

## Chapter 5

Poor Rip humbly assured him that he meant no harm. "I came in search of my friends. They used to sit outside this inn."

"Well, who are they? Name them."

Rip thought a moment, and asked, "Where's Nicholas Vedder?"

There was a silence for a little while. An old man replied, in a thin, piping voice, "Nicholas Vedder! Why, he is dead and gone these eighteen years! There was a wooden tombstone in the churchyard. It told all about him, but that's rotten and gone too."

"Where's Brom Dutcher?"

"Oh, he went off to the army in the beginning of the war. Some say he was killed at the storming of Stony Point. Others say he drowned in a storm at sea. I don't know. He never came back again."

"Where's Van Bummel, the schoolmaster?"

"He went off to the wars too. He was a great militia general. He is now in Congress."

Rip's heart died away at hearing of these sad changes in his home and friends. He was finding himself thus alone in the world. Every answer puzzled him too. There were of such enormous lapses of time. There were events he could not understand: war-Congress-Stony Point. He had no courage to ask after any more friends.

Finally, Rip cried out in despair, "Does nobody here know Rip Van Winkle?"

"Oh, Rip Van Winkle!" exclaimed two or three, "Oh, to be sure! That's Rip Van Winkle yonder, leaning against the tree."

Rip looked. He saw a man that looked just like himself, as he went up the mountain. Apparently the man was as lazy and certainly as ragged. The poor fellow was now completely confounded. He doubted his own identity. Was he himself or another man? In the midst of his bewilderment, the self-important acting man demanded to know his name.

"Only God knows," exclaimed Rip Van Winkle, at his wit's end. "I'm not myself. I'm somebody else. That's me leaning against the tree-no-that's somebody else got into my shoes. I was myself last night. I fell asleep on the mountain. They've changed my gun. Everything has changed. I'm changed. I can't tell what my name is, or who I am!"

The bystanders began now to look at each other. They nodded, winked, and tapped their fingers against their foreheads. There was a whisper about securing the gun. The old man might be dangerous. At the very suggestion, the self-important man moved to a safe distance at the back of the crowd.

At this critical moment a pretty, young woman pressed through the crowd. She wanted a peep at the gray-bearded man. She had a chubby child in her arms. The baby was frightened at his looks and began to cry.

"Hush, Rip," cried she, "hush, my little child. The old man won't hurt you."

The name of the child, the air of the mother, the tone of her voice, all awakened a train of recollections in his mind.

"What is your name, my good woman?" asked he.

"Judith Gardener."

"And your father's name?"

"Ah! Poor man, Rip Van Winkle was his name. It's been twenty years since he went away from home with his gun. He has never been heard of since. His dog came home without him. He may have shot himself. Perhaps he was carried away by the Indians. Nobody can tell. I was then but a little girl."

Rip had but one question to ask. He asked nervously, "Where's your mother?"

"Oh, she too had died but a short time since. She broke a blood-vessel in a fit of anger at a New England peddler."

There was a drop of comfort for Rip. The honest man could contain himself no longer. He caught his daughter and her child in his arms.

"I am your father!" cried he-"Young Rip Van Winkle once-old Rip Van Winkle now! Does nobody know poor old Rip Van Winkle?"

All stood amazed, until an old woman came out from among the crowd. She put her hand to her brow. She peered at his face for a moment and exclaimed, "Sure enough! It is Rip Van Winkle. It is himself! Welcome home again, old neighbor. Why, where have you been these twenty long years?"

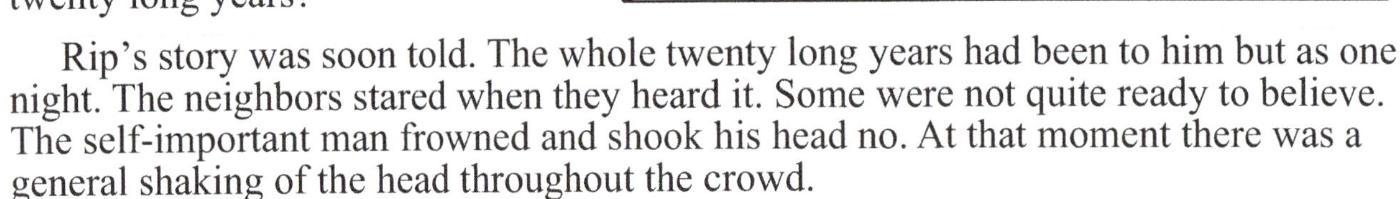

Rip's story was soon told. The whole twenty long years had been to him but as one night. The neighbors stared when they heard it. Some were not quite ready to believe. The self-important man frowned and shook his head no. At that moment there was a general shaking of the head throughout the crowd.

It was determined, however, to take the opinion of old Peter Vanderdonk. He was seen slowly advancing up the road. Peter was the most ancient inhabitant of the village. He was well versed in all the wonderful events and traditions of the neighborhood.

Peter recollected Rip at once. He assured the people that it was a fact, handed down from his ancestor the historian, that the Catskill Mountains had always been haunted by strange beings. The great Hendrick Hudson, the first discoverer of the river and country, kept a kind of vigil there every twenty years. With his crew of the ship, the Half-moon, he would revisit the area.

Peter said his father had once seen them in their old Dutch dresses playing at ninepins in a hollow of the mountain. He himself had heard one summer afternoon, the sound of their balls, like distant peals of thunder.

To make a long story short, the crowd broke up. They returned to the more important concerns of the election. Rip's daughter took him home to live with her. She had a snug, well-furnished house. She was married to a cheery farmer. Rip remembered him as one of the children that used to climb upon his back.

Rip's son and heir was employed to work on the farm. Like his father, he had no interest in working on the farm. Rip now resumed his old walks and habits. He soon found many of his former friends. They all seemed too old for him. Rip preferred making friends among the younger villagers. They soon became very fond of him too.

Having nothing to do at home, Rip took his place once more on the bench at the inn door. He was reverenced as one of the fathers of the village. He could tell all about the old times "before the war."

It was some time before he could understand the strange events that had taken place during his sleep. There had been a revolutionary war. The country had thrown off the yoke of old England. Instead of being a subject to his Majesty George the Third, he was now a free citizen of the United States.

Rip in fact, was no politician. The changes of states and empires made but no difference to him. There was only one government that made him suffer. That was the nagging ruler of his household.

Happily that was at an end. He was free of the tyranny of Dame Van Winkle. He could go wherever he liked. He could do as he pleased. Whenever her name was mentioned, however, he cowered and looked over his shoulder.

He used to tell his story to every stranger that arrived at Mr. Doolittle's hotel. He was observed, at first, to vary on some points every time he told it. That was to be expected after sleeping twenty years. It at last settled down precisely to the tale I have told. Every man, woman, and child in the neighborhood knew it by heart.

Some always doubted the reality of it. They insisted that Rip had been out of his head. The old Dutch inhabitants, however, almost all believed it. Even to this day when they hear a thunder-storm of a summer afternoon about the Catskill they say Hendrick Hudson and his crew are at their game of ninepins. It is a common wish of all hen-pecked husbands in the neighborhood for a drink of Hendrick Hudson's mysterious drink. They envy the peaceful sleep of Rip Van Winkle.

# The Emperor's New Clothes

Original Story by Hans Christian Anderson

Adapted by Brian Davis
Illustrations by Ron Wheeler



*The Emperor's New Clothes* was written by Hans Christian Anderson. The story was first published in 1837.

What do you do when you just don't have anything magnificent to wear?

If you're an emperor who cares too much about clothing, you might just spend a fortune only to be embarrassed.

## Chapter 1

Many years ago there was an Emperor, who was so excessively fond of new clothes. He spent all his money on them. He cared nothing about his soldiers. He cared nothing for the theatre. He only liked riding in his carriage for the sake of showing off his new clothes. He had a costume for every hour in the day.

Most kings or emperors would spend time with their officials. They planned how to run the kingdom. They made plans to help the people. Here one always said, "The Emperor is in his dressing-room."

Life was very merry in the great town where he lived. Hosts of strangers came to visit it every day. Among them one day were two swindlers. They claimed that they were skilled weavers. They said that they knew how to weave the most beautiful clothing imaginable. The colors and patterns were unusually fine. The clothing was special in another way. The clothes were made of material that had a very peculiar quality. They became invisible to every person who was not fit for the office he held.

"Those must be splendid clothes," thought the Emperor. "By wearing them I will learn about those who work for me. I should be able to discover which men in my kingdom are unfit for their posts. I shall distinguish the wise men from the fools. Yes, I certainly must order some clothing to be woven for me."

He paid the two swindlers a lot of money in advance. They agreed to begin their work at once.

They did put up two looms and pretended to weave. In reality they had nothing whatever upon their shuttles. At the outset, they asked for a quantity of the finest silk and the purest gold thread. They put the valuable materials into their own bags. All the while they pretended to work away at the empty looms far into the night.

"I should like to know how those weavers are getting on with the clothing," thought the Emperor. He felt a little strange about the clothing. He was concerned that he might discover trusted officials were unfit. It concerned him that he couldn't tell without the clothing.

The emperor certainly thought that he need have no fears for himself. He considered himself quite fit for his office. Still, he thought he would send somebody else first to see how it was getting on. Everybody in the town knew what wonderful power the clothing possessed. Every one was anxious to see how stupid his neighbor was.

"I will send my faithful old minister to the weavers," thought the Emperor. "He will be best able to see how the stuff looks. He is a clever man. No one fulfills his duties better than he does!"

So the good old minister went into the weaving room. The two swindlers sat working at the empty loom.

The old minister opened his eyes very wide. It didn't help. He thought to himself, "Why, I can't see a thing!" But he took care not to say so. He didn't want to be thought of as a fool.

Both the swindlers begged him to be good enough to step a little nearer. They asked if he liked the pattern and beautiful coloring. They pointed to the empty loom. The poor old minister stared as hard as he could. He could not see anything, for of course there was nothing to see.

"Could it be?" thought he. "Is it possible that I am a fool? I have never thought so. Nobody must know it. Am I not fit for my post? I should never admit that I cannot see the cloth."

"Well, Sir, you don't say anything about the cloth," said the swindler. "Do you like it? Is it something the emperor will like?" He asked as he continued to pretend to weave.

"Oh, it is beautiful! Quite charming!" said the old minister. He looked through his spectacles. "This pattern and these colors are wonderful! I will certainly tell the Emperor that the cloth pleases me very much."

"We are delighted to hear you say so," said the swindlers. "See the majestic purple, the royal blues, the rich golden hues. We can't wait for the emperor to wear them."

They gave names to all the colors and patterns. The old minister paid great attention to what they said. He wanted to repeat it when he got home to the emperor.

Then the swindlers went on to demand more money. They wanted more silk, and more gold. The swindlers claimed they must have it to continue their work. They wouldn't use any of it. Instead, they put it all into their own pockets. Not a single thread was ever put into the loom. They went on as before, weaving at the empty loom.

The Emperor soon sent another faithful official. He was to see how the clothing was progressing. He wanted to know if it would be ready soon. The same thing happened to him as to the minister. He looked and looked. All he saw was the empty loom. He could see no cloth on it at all.

"Is not this a beautiful piece of cloth?" said both the swindlers. They told the official about the rich colors. They explained the beautiful patterns. Of course, there was nothing to be seen.

"I know I am not a fool!" thought the man. "So it must be that I am unfit for my good post! It is very strange, though! However, I must not let anyone know!"

So he praised the cloth he did not see. The official assured them of his delight in the beautiful colors. He commended the originality of the design.

"It is absolutely charming! You have nothing like it," he reported to the Emperor. Everybody in the town was talking about this splendid cloth.

## Chapter 2

Days and days went by. The swindlers continued to collect more money and expensive materials from the emperor's officials. Everyone seemed to be impressed with how hard they worked. The swindlers, of course, were doing nothing but becoming richer.

Now the Emperor thought he would like to see it while it was still on the loom. He was accompanied by a number of selected courtiers. Among them were the two faithful officials who had already seen the imaginary cloth. He went to visit the crafty impostors. They were working away as hard as ever at the empty loom.

"It is magnificent!" said both the honest officials. "Only see, your Majesty, what a design! What colors!"

And they pointed to the empty loom. They thought no doubt the others could see the stuff. They knew the others were not fools. They began to doubt themselves. Both officials were determined not to be discovered as fools.

"What!" thought the Emperor; "I see nothing at all! This is terrible! Am I a fool? Am I not fit to be Emperor? Why, nothing worse could happen to me!" That was what he thought. It was not what he said.

"Oh, it is beautiful!" said the Emperor. "It has my highest approval!" He nodded his satisfaction as he gazed at the empty loom. Nothing would make him to say that he could not see anything.

All the emperor's officials gazed and gazed. They saw nothing more than all the others. However, they all exclaimed with his Majesty, "It is very beautiful!" They advised him to wear a suit made of this wonderful cloth. He could wear it in the parade at the upcoming festival.

"It is magnificent! Gorgeous! Excellent!" went from mouth to mouth. They were all equally delighted with it. The Emperor gave each of the swindlers medals of knighthood. They were to wear them with honor. He gave them the title of "Gentlemen weavers."

The swindlers sat up the whole night before the day of the parade. They burned sixteen candles. The swindlers wanted all to see that they were anxious to complete the emperor's clothing. They pretended to take the cloth off the loom. They cut it out in the air with a huge pair of scissors. They stitched away with needles without any thread in them.

At last they declared, "Now the Emperor's new clothes are ready!"

The Emperor, with his grandest courtiers, went to them himself. Both the swindlers raised one arm in the air. They pretended to hold something.

One of the swindlers said, "See, these are the trousers. This is the coat. Here is the cape!" and so on. "It is as light as a spider's web. One might think one had nothing on. That is the very beauty of it!"

"Yes!" said all the courtiers "It is so beautiful." In truth, they could not see anything. There was nothing to see.

"Will your imperial majesty be graciously pleased to take off your clothes?" asked the swindlers. "You may put on the new ones. You must see yourself in front of this great mirror."

The Emperor took off his cape. He took off his shirt. He took off his trousers. He was wearing nothing but his underwear. The impostors pretended to give him one article of clothing after the other.

The emperor pretended to take them with great admiration. They pretended to fasten something round his waist. They pretended to tie on the cape. The swindlers pretended it was long and flowing. They stood back a few feet and pretended to lift up the ends.

The Emperor turned round and round in front of the mirror. The swindlers turned with him to keep the pretend cape from twisting. "We must be careful not to wrinkle it," they explained. All the officials nodded in agreement.

"How well his majesty looks in the new clothes! How becoming they are!" cried all the people round. "What a design, and what colors! They are most gorgeous robes!"

"The canopy is waiting outside which is to be carried over your majesty in the procession," said the leader of the parade. "The people of the village are anxious to see your fine clothes."

"Well, I am quite ready," said the Emperor. "Don't the clothes fit well?" He turned round again in front of the mirror. He pretended to be looking at his grand things. He wanted everyone to understand that he was not a fool.

The servants who were to carry the long cape stepped forward. They stooped and pretended to lift it from the ground with both hands. They walked along with their hands in the air. The servants dared not let it appear that they could not see anything.

Then the Emperor walked along in the parade under the gorgeous canopy. Everybody in the streets and at the windows exclaimed, "How beautiful the Emperor's new clothes are! What a splendid cape! And they fit to perfection!" Nobody would let it appear that he could see nothing. That would mean he would not be fit for his post. He would be seen as a fool.

The crowds cheered in approval. The emperor marched forth proudly. None of the Emperor's clothes had been so popular before.

"But he has got nothing on!" said a little child.

"Oh, listen to the innocent child," said its father. One person whispered to the other what the child had said. "He has nothing on. A child says he has nothing on!"

"But he has nothing on!" at last cried all the people.

The Emperor turned red in embarrassment. He knew it was true. Still, he thought "the parade must go on now." He was as determined as ever to pretend the clothing was real. The one thing the emperor could not accept was that he was a fool. All the officials pretended with him.

Original Story by Hans Christian Anderson

Edited by Brian Davis
Illustrations by Brian Davis



*The Ugly Duckling* was written by Hans Christian Anderson. The story was first published in 1844.

When the last egg of the mother duck hatches she is in for a big surprise.

*The Ugly Duckling* is a story about acceptance of others and how beauty can sometimes become too important.

## Chapter 1
## A Bad Egg?

It was lovely summer weather in the country. The golden corn, the green oats, and the haystacks piled up in the meadows looked beautiful. The stork walking about on his long red legs chattered in the Egyptian language. He had learned it from his mother.

The corn-fields and meadows were surrounded by large forests, in the midst of which were deep pools. It was, indeed, delightful to walk about in the country. In a sunny spot stood a pleasant, old farm-house close by a deep river. From the house down to the water side grew great burdock leaves, so high, that under the tallest of them a little child could stand upright.

The spot was as wild as the center of a thick wood. In this snug retreat sat a duck on her nest, watching for her young brood to hatch. She was beginning to get tired of her task. The little ones were a long time coming out of their shells, and she seldom had any visitors. The other ducks liked much better to swim about in the river than to climb the slippery banks and sit under a burdock leaf to have a gossip with her.

At length one shell cracked, and then another. From each egg came a living creature that lifted its head and cried, "Peep, peep."

"Quack, quack," said the mother.

They all quacked as well as they could, and looked about them on every side at the large green leaves. Their mother allowed them to look as much as they liked because green is good for the eyes.

"How large the world is," said the young ducks, when they found how much more room they now had than while they were inside the egg-shell.

"Do you imagine this is the whole world?" asked the mother; "Wait till you have seen the garden. It stretches far beyond that to the parson's field. I have never ventured to such a distance. Are you all out of your shells?" she continued, rising; "No, I declare, the largest egg lies there still. I wonder how long this is to last. I am quite tired of it," she seated herself again on the nest.

"Well, how are you getting on?" asked an old duck, who paid her a visit.

"One egg is not hatched yet," said the duck. "It will not break. But just look at all the others, are they not the prettiest little ducklings you ever saw? They are the image of their father, who is so unkind. He never comes to see."

"Let me see the egg that will not break," said the duck. "I have no doubt it is a turkey's egg. I was persuaded to hatch some once and after all my care and trouble with the young ones. They were afraid of the water. I quacked and clucked, but all to no purpose. I could not get them to venture in. Let me look at the egg. Yes, that is a turkey's egg. Take my advice, leave it where it is and teach the other children to swim."

"I think I will sit on it a little while longer," said the duck, "as I have sat so long already, a few days will be nothing."

"Please yourself," said the old duck, and she went away.

At last the large egg broke, and a young one crept forth crying, "Peep, peep." It was very large and ugly.

The duck stared at it and exclaimed, "It is very large and not at all like the others. I wonder if it really is a turkey. We shall soon find it out, however, when we go to the water. It must go in, if I have to push it myself."

On the next day the weather was delightful. The sun shone brightly on the green burdock leaves, so the mother duck took her young brood down to the water. She jumped in with a splash. "Quack, quack," cried she.

One after another the little ducklings jumped in. The water closed over their heads, but they came up again in an instant. The ducklings swam about quite prettily with their legs paddling under them as easily as possible. The ugly duckling was also in the water swimming with them.

"Oh," said the mother, "that is not a turkey; how well he uses his legs, and how upright he holds himself! He is my own child, and he is not so very ugly after all if you look at him properly. Quack, quack! Come with me now, I will take you into grand society, and introduce you to the farmyard, but you must keep close to me or you may be trodden upon. Above all, beware of the cat."

When they reached the farmyard, there was a great disturbance; two families were fighting for an eel's head, which, after all, was carried off by the cat.

"See, children, that is the way of the world," said the mother duck, whetting her beak, for she would have liked the eel's head herself. "Come, now, use your legs, and let me see how well you can behave. You must bow your heads prettily to that old duck yonder. She is the highest born of them all, and has Spanish blood, therefore, she is well off. Don't you see she has a red flag tied to her leg, which is something very grand and a great honor for a duck? It shows that everyone is anxious not to lose her, as she can be recognized both by man and beast. Come, now, don't turn your toes, a well-bred duckling spreads his feet wide apart, just like his father and mother, in this way; now bend your neck, and say 'quack.'"

The ducklings did as they were bid, but the other duck stared, and said, "Look, here comes another brood, as if there were not enough of us already! And what a strange looking object one of them is. We don't want him here," and then one flew out and bit him in the neck.

## Chapter 2
## Barnyard Bullies

The mother duck did not like seeing one of her young ducklings getting bullied.

"Let him alone," said the mother; "he is not doing any harm."

"Yes, but he is so big and ugly," said the spiteful duck "and, therefore, he must be turned out."

"The others are very pretty children," said the old duck, with the rag on her leg, "all but that one. I wish his mother could improve him a little."

"That is impossible, your grace," replied the mother. "He is not pretty; but he has a very good disposition and swims as well or even better than the others. I think he will grow up pretty, and perhaps be smaller. He has remained too long in the egg, and therefore his figure is not properly formed." Then she stroked his neck and smoothed the feathers, saying, "It is a drake, and therefore not of so much consequence. I think he will grow up strong and able to take care of himself."

"The other ducklings are graceful enough," said the old duck. "Now make yourself at home, and if you can find an eel's head, you can bring it to me."

And so they made themselves comfortable, but the poor duckling, who had crept out of his shell last of all, and looked so ugly, was bitten and pushed and made fun of, not only by the ducks, but by all the poultry.

"He is too big," they all said, and the turkey cock, who had been born into the world with spurs, and fancied himself really an emperor. He puffed himself out like a ship in full sail, and flew at the duckling. He became quite red in the head with passion, so that the poor little duckling did not know where to go.

He was quite miserable because he was so ugly and laughed at by the whole farmyard. So it went on from day to day till it got worse and worse. The poor duckling was driven about by everyone; even his brothers and sisters were unkind to him and would say, "Ah, you ugly creature, I wish the cat would get you,"

His mother said she wished he had never been born. The ducks pecked him, the chickens beat him, and the girl who fed the poultry kicked him with her feet. So at last he ran away, frightening the little birds in the hedge as he flew over the nests.

"They are afraid of me because I am ugly," he said. So he closed his eyes, and flew still farther, until he came out on a large moor, inhabited by wild ducks. Here he remained the whole night, feeling very tired and sorrowful.

In the morning, when the wild ducks rose in the air, they stared at their new comrade. "What sort of a duck are you?" they all said, coming round him.

He bowed to them and was as polite as he could be, but he did not reply to their question.

"You are exceedingly ugly," said the wild ducks, "but that will not matter if you do not want to marry one of our family."

Poor thing! He had no thoughts of marriage. All he wanted was permission to lie among the rushes and drink some of the water on the moor. After he had been on the moor two days, there came two wild geese, or rather goslings, for they had not been out of the egg long and were very saucy.

"Listen, friend," said one of them to the duckling, "you are so ugly that we like you very well. Will you go with us and become a bird of passage? Not far from here is another moor, in which there are some pretty wild geese, all unmarried. It is a chance for you to get a wife; you may be lucky, ugly as you are."

"Pop, pop," sounded in the air, and the two wild geese fell dead among the rushes, and the water was tinged with blood. "Pop, pop," echoed far and wide in the distance, and whole flocks of wild geese rose up from the rushes.

The sound continued from every direction, for the sportsmen surrounded the moor, and some were even seated on branches of trees, overlooking the rushes. The blue smoke from the guns rose like clouds over the dark trees. As it floated away across the water, a number of sporting dogs bounded in among the rushes, which bent beneath them wherever they went. How they terrified the poor duckling!

He turned away his head to hide it under his wing. At the same moment a large terrible dog passed quite near him. His jaws were open, his tongue hung from his mouth, and his eyes glared fearfully. He thrust his nose close to the duckling, showing his sharp teeth, and then, "splash, splash," he went into the water without touching him.

"Oh," sighed the duckling, "how thankful I am for being so ugly. Even a dog will not bite me."

And so he lay quite still, while the shot rattled through the rushes and gun after gun was fired over him. It was late in the day before all became quiet. Even then the poor young thing did not dare to move. He waited quietly for several hours, and then, after looking carefully around him, hastened away from the moor as fast as he could.

He ran over field and meadow till a storm arose, and he could hardly struggle against it. Towards evening, he reached a poor little cottage that seemed ready to fall, and only remained standing because it could not decide on which side to fall first. The storm continued so violent that the duckling could go no farther.

## Chapter 3
## A Cold Winter

He sat down by the cottage, and then he noticed that the door was not quite closed in consequence of one of the hinges having given way. There was, therefore, a narrow opening near the bottom large enough for him to slip through, which he did very quietly. It would provide him shelter for the night.

A woman, a tom cat, and a hen lived in this cottage. The tom cat, whom the mistress called, "My little son," was a great favorite. He could raise his back, and purr, and could even throw out sparks from his fur if it were stroked the wrong way.

The hen had very short legs, so she was called "Chickie short legs." She laid good eggs, and her mistress loved her as if she had been her own child. In the morning, the strange visitor was discovered, and the tom cat began to purr, and the hen to cluck.

"What is that noise about?" said the old woman, looking round the room, but her sight was not very good; therefore, when she saw the duckling she thought it must be a fat duck that had strayed from home.

"Oh what a prize!" she exclaimed, "I hope it is not a drake, for then I shall have some duck's eggs. I must wait and see."

So the duckling was allowed to remain on trial for three weeks, but there were no eggs. Now the tom cat was the master of the house, and the hen was mistress, and they always said, "We and the world," for they believed themselves to be half the world, and the better half too. The duckling thought that others might hold a different opinion on the subject, but the hen would not listen to such doubts.

"Can you lay eggs?" she asked.

"No," answered the duckling.

"Then have the goodness to hold your tongue."

"Can you raise your back, or purr, or throw out sparks?" said the tom cat.

"No," replied the duckling.

"Then you have no right to express an opinion when sensible people are speaking."

So the duckling sat in a corner, feeling very low spirited, till the sunshine and the fresh air came into the room through the open door. Then he began to feel such a great longing for a swim on the water, that he could not help telling the hen.

"What an absurd idea," said the hen. "You have nothing else to do, therefore you have foolish fancies. If you could purr or lay eggs, they would pass away."

"But it is so delightful to swim about on the water," said the duckling, "and so refreshing to feel it close over your head, while you dive down to the bottom."

"Delightful, indeed!" said the hen, "why you must be crazy! Ask the cat, he is the cleverest animal I know. Ask him how he would like to swim about on the water, or to dive under it, for I will not speak of my own opinion. Ask our mistress, the old woman-there is no one in the world more clever than she is. Do you think she would like to swim, or to let the water close over her head?"

"You don't understand me," said the duckling.

"We don't understand you? Who can understand you, I wonder? Do you consider yourself more clever than the cat, or the old woman? I will say nothing of myself. Don't imagine such nonsense, child, and thank your good fortune that you have been received here. Are you not in a warm room, and in society from which you may learn something? But you are a chatterer, and your company is not very agreeable. Believe me; I speak only for your own good. I may tell you unpleasant truths, but that is a proof of my friendship. I advise you, therefore, to lay eggs, and learn to purr as quickly as possible."

"I believe I must go out into the world again," said the duckling.

"Yes, do," said the hen.

So the duckling left the cottage, and soon found water on which it could swim and dive. The duckling was avoided by all other animals because of its ugly appearance. Autumn came, and the leaves in the forest turned to orange and gold. Then as winter approached, the wind caught them as they fell and whirled them in the cold air. The clouds, heavy with hail and snow-flakes, hung low in the sky.

The raven stood on the ferns crying, "Croak, croak." It made one shiver with cold to look at him. All this was very sad for the poor little duckling. One evening, just as the sun set amid radiant clouds, there came a large flock of beautiful birds out of the bushes. The duckling had never seen any like them before.

They were swans, and they curved their graceful necks, while their soft plumage shown with dazzling whiteness. They uttered a singular cry, as they spread their glorious wings and flew away from those cold regions to warmer countries across the sea.

As they mounted higher and higher in the air, the ugly little duckling felt quite a strange sensation as he watched them. He whirled himself in the water like a wheel, stretched out his neck towards them, and uttered a cry so strange that it frightened himself. Could he ever forget those beautiful, happy birds? When at last they were out of his sight, he dove under the water, and rose again almost beside himself with excitement.

He knew not the names of these birds, nor where they had flown, but he felt towards them as he had never felt for any other bird in the world. He was not envious of these beautiful creatures, but wished to be as lovely as they.

Poor ugly creature, how gladly he would have lived even with the ducks had they only given him encouragement. The winter grew colder and colder. He had to swim about on the water to keep it from freezing, but every night the space on which he swam became smaller and smaller. At length it froze so hard that the ice in the water crackled as he moved. The duckling had to paddle with his legs as well as he could, to keep the space from closing up. He became exhausted at last, and lay still and helpless, frozen fast in the ice.

## Chapter 4
## A Beautiful Reflection

Early in the morning, a peasant, who was passing by, saw what had happened. He broke the ice in pieces with his wooden shoe, and carried the duckling home to his wife. The warmth revived the poor little creature, but when the children wanted to play with him, the duckling thought they would do him some harm.

He started up in terror, fluttered into the milk-pan, and splashed the milk about the room. Then the woman clapped her hands, which frightened him still more. He flew first into the butter-cask, then into the meal-tub, and out again. What a condition he was in!

The woman screamed, and struck at him with the tongs; the children laughed and screamed, and tumbled over each other, in their efforts to catch him; but luckily he escaped. The door stood open; the poor creature could just manage to slip out among the bushes, and lie down quite exhausted in the newly fallen snow.

It would be very sad, were I to relate all the misery and privations which the poor little duckling endured during the hard winter. When it had passed, he found himself lying one morning in a moor, amongst the rushes. He felt the warm sun shining, and heard the lark singing, and saw that all around was beautiful spring. Then the young bird felt that his wings were strong, as he flapped them against his sides, and rose high into the air.

They bore him onwards, until he found himself in a large garden, before he well knew how it had happened. The apple-trees were in full blossom, and the fragrant elders bent their long green branches down to the stream which wound round a smooth lawn. Everything looked beautiful, in the freshness of early spring.

From a thicket close by came three beautiful white swans, rustling their feathers, and swimming lightly over the smooth water. The duckling remembered the lovely birds, and felt more strangely unhappy than ever. He wished he could turn and fly away. Nevertheless, he was drawn to the beautiful creatures.

"I will fly to those royal birds," he exclaimed, "and they will kill me because I am so ugly, and dare to approach them; but it does not matter: better be killed by them than pecked by the ducks, beaten by the hens, pushed about by the maiden who feeds the poultry, or starved with hunger in the winter."

Then he flew to the water, and swam towards the beautiful swans. The moment they spied the stranger, they rushed to meet him with outstretched wings.

"Kill me," said the poor bird, and he bent his head down to the surface of the water, and awaited death.

But what did he see in the clear stream below? His own image; no longer a dark, gray bird, ugly and disagreeable to look at, but a graceful and beautiful swan. To be born in a duck's nest, in a farmyard, is of no consequence to a bird, if it is hatched from a swan's egg. He now felt glad at having suffered sorrow and trouble because it enabled him to enjoy so much better all the pleasure and happiness around him; for the great swans swam round the new-comer, and stroked his neck with their beaks, as a welcome.

Into the garden presently came some little children, and threw bread and cake into the water.

"See," cried the youngest, "there is a new one;" and the rest were delighted, and ran to their father and mother, dancing and clapping their hands, and shouting joyously, "There is another swan come; a new one has arrived."

Then they threw more bread and cake into the water, and said, "The new one is the most beautiful of all; he is so young and pretty." And the old swans bowed their heads before him.

Then he felt quite ashamed, and hid his head under his wing; for he did not know what to do, he was so happy, and yet not at all proud. He had been persecuted and despised for his ugliness. Now he heard them say he was the most beautiful of all the birds. Even the elder-tree bent down its bows into the water before him, and the sun shone warm and bright.

Then he rustled his feathers, curved his slender neck, and cried joyfully, from the depths of his heart, "I never dreamed of such happiness as this, while I was an ugly duckling."

You can make poetry more interesting by emphasizing sounds and word patterns in different ways.

**Alliteration** uses the repetition of consonant sounds at the beginning of each word or each stressed syllable in a line of verse. Many words can begin with the same sound, or as few as two words. Look for examples of alliteration in the poems *Wiggle Worm Crook* and *Snail Spaghetti*.

## Alliteration

### *Wiggle Worm Crook*

Did the big blue bass bite the baited hook?  
The fisherman hoped when the line shook  
But there would be no lunch for him to cook  
For the line was snipped  
by that wise, wiggle worm crook

### *Snail Spaghetti*

The silly, slimy snail slurped Sue's spaghetti  
Sue screamed at such a sickening sight  
"Don't be sad,"  
sighed the sorry snail  
"I will certainly save you  
at least one saucy bite."

**Assonance** is also the repetition of sounds. The repetition of vowel sounds in a line of verse is called assonance. The vowel sound does not have to be at the beginning of the word. It does not have to be spelled the same way in the words. Look for assonance in the poem, *Ape Grapes*.

## Assonance

### *Ape Grapes*

The great ape ate eighty-eight grapes  
The great ape now has a major belly ache  
The great ape complained,  
"Where is my dainty waist?"  
"Those days are gone,"  
he heard a blue jay say  
"It's now Great Ape's  
grapes storage space."

# Sounds of Poetry

**Onomatopoeia** (on-uh-mat-uh-pee-uh) is the term for using words to imitate sounds made by objects or animals, such as "moo" for a cow's sound or "ding-dong" for a bell ringing. Read the poem *The Broken Egg* and find examples of onomatopoeia.

## Onomatopoeia

***The Broken Egg***

"Cackle!" went the hen
"Splat!" went the egg.
"Oh!" groaned the farmer
"Yahoo!" exclaimed the rat
"Slurp!" went its breakfast
"Burp"

**Repetition** of words or phrases in a poem can give the reader a sense of rhythm, such as the first line of the poem *The Great Army*. Repetition can also add emphasis. Look at the third line of the poem. Repetition adds an emphasis that the ant army is unstoppable. Look for other examples of repetition in the poem. Is the repetition there for emphasis or rhythm?

## Repetition

***The Great Army***

The ants are marching, marching, marching on
An army moving, moving, moving on
Nothing is too big, too big for them all
For with this great army
Fort Picnic will fall!
With this great army
Bananas and all

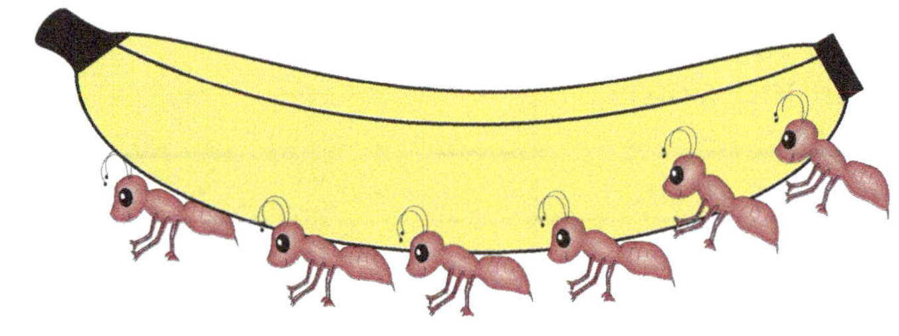

# Future Me

by Brian Davis
illustrations by Ron Wheeler



Do you know anyone into video games? When Adam gets a new game he has a chance to really get into it.

Find out what happens when he helps out the mysterious Professor Omega who is running for his life!

## Chapter 1
## Isosceles on the Run

"Whoa, now that's amazing," said Adam as he stared back at his feet while lying on the floor.

You wouldn't think tripping over a scooter would be amazing. It's not in and of itself, but if you had just made yourself do it in a video game, you might think otherwise. That's what happened to Adam.

Adam was still trying to get a feel for the controls on the game. He was navigating his character around the cyber-room when it tripped and fell. At that moment a siren outside the window caught his attention. That's when Adam hopped up to race across the room. He tripped just like the character in the video game.

By the time Adam got up the sirens had faded. He went back to the computer and started playing again. He was drawn to the game for some reason. It didn't seem that fun at first, but if Professor Omega made it, the game had to be filled with amazing things.

Adam had never met anyone quite as creative as Professor Omega. They probably would never have met if it hadn't been for Isosceles. The professor who lived in the apartment below Adam's always kept to himself. It wasn't that he was unfriendly; it was just that he had a very busy mind that never seemed to slow down.

The only friend the professor made time for before meeting Adam was his cat, Isosceles. The day the lady with the loud yapping dogs moved in, the cat was not happy. Isosceles was napping peacefully on the fire escape. When the dogs caught a whiff of cat, they were out the window. The woman screamed at first thinking her pets had just jumped out a fourth story apartment.

Fortunately for the dogs, the fire escape provided a safe landing spot. The dogs didn't stay there long. They bounded up the steps to catch the napping feline. Between the screaming woman and the two dogs zipping up the step, the sleepy cat was terrorized.

It bounded right up to Adam's apartment and in through the window, knocking his baseball trophies to the floor in the process. Adam wasn't quite fast enough to close the window before the dogs reached it.

Isosceles, trapped in the room, didn't know what to think. The terrified cat sprung around the room jumping from the bed to shelves to a dresser. Between sharp teeth and claws Adam was more concerned for his own safety. The dogs yapped and gave chase. Adam bolted from the room and trapped the animals inside.

Adam had seen the cat around. He knew where it belonged. The boy raced down the stairs and knocked on the professor's door. He was quite winded and red in the face when the professor opened the door.

"Crazy dogs…wild cat…my room!" panted Adam.

Those were the first words he had ever spoken to Professor Omega. It seemed to be enough for the professor. The two of them raced back up the stairs. By now, the new lady was also in pursuit. Between the screeching of the cat, the screaming lady, and the barking of the dogs everyone on the sixth floor knew something was wrong.

They all almost collided with Adam's mom as she stepped off the elevator. Her arms were filled with bags of groceries. At first she got a scowl on her face as Adam ran by and didn't even attempt to help her. Then she noticed all the commotion and joined in the pursuit while trying to not spill the bags.

By the time they reached Adam's room, they heard sounds of things crashing to the floor. Suddenly, there was a low growl. It was a cat growl, not a dog growl. The dogs must have had Isosceles cornered. That was quickly followed by a loud yelping.

Adam opened his door and saw the scratches on the noses of the dogs. The new lady pushed past him and picked up her precious pets.

"My poor babies!" she cried. "What a horrid cat!"

With that she angrily turned and left the apartment. Professor Omega timidly peeked into the room. He sighed deeply and ran his hand though his gray, curly hair. Isosceles sat in the corner and calmly licked her front paws.

The professor turned toward Adam's mom, "I'm so sorry. I'll help clean up, and if there are any damages…"

"It wasn't the cat's fault," Adam said to his mom. "Those dogs chased her up here. She was just trying to escape."

Adam didn't know what to expect from his mom. He studied her face, but couldn't get a good read. Was she about to explode? The professor could feel the tension too. He looked like he was ready to take cover at any instant.

Suddenly, she smiled and shook her head, "I've never seen two more pitiful expressions." She looked around the room. "Believe it or not, I've seen it looking worse."

The professor smiled, "We've been neighbors all this time and we haven't really met. My name is Alfred Omega. I live in the apartment right below yours."

"I've seen you around," said Adam's mom as picked up the groceries to carry them to the kitchen.

The professor automatically grabbed a bag and followed. Adam noticed that his mom didn't seem to mind. Normally, she didn't like strangers in her apartment, especially strange men. There was something about the professor that made her lighten up a bit. It was a side of his mom that Adam hadn't seen in quite some time. After his dad left, she had been pretty unhappy.

Alfred Omega made good on his promise to clean up the mess. Adam and the professor worked for the next few hours. When they were finished, Adam's room looked better than it had ever looked. It looked better than Adam could have ever imagined it could look. The professor had quite a knack for organizing.

Adam's mom was grateful too. She had a nice pot of spaghetti ready after the room was cleaned. She even placed a bowl of milk on the floor for Isosceles. The professor, who rarely had a home cooked meal, was thrilled.

Even though the professor was at least thirty years older than Adam's mom, he and Adam's mom had a lot in common. They both studied computer science in college. They liked many of the same things. Most of all, they both needed a friend to talk to. The professor and Adam's mom laughed and talked well into the evening. Adam and Isosceles curled up on the couch and fell asleep.

In the weeks that followed, Adam, his mom, and the professor had many more evenings like this. It was good to have neighbors that were also friends.

## Chapter 2
## The Drop-off

So how did Adam get this mysterious video game?

It all started earlier that afternoon on his way home from school. Adam was gliding down the sidewalk on his scooter. His mom had told him to be careful of pedestrians. Generally, Adam was mindful of people on the sidewalk.

When they pop out of nowhere running full speed, it's a little difficult to react quickly enough. Before he knew it, Adam and the professor were tumbling to the sidewalk. Before Adam could apologize, Professor Omega dragged Adam into the nearest building.

Adam had never seen the professor act this strangely, and the professor wasn't the most normal guy around. Alfred Omega kept staring out the window. He seemed terrified as a black SUV rolled slowly down the street.

The professor pressed something into Adam's pants pocket.

"If anything happens to me, call the number on this card," said the professor.

Adam looked at the card. It was a business card, but was strange in one way. It didn't have the name of a person or business on it. It was simply a printed phone number.

Just then, the SUV returned.

"I've got to run now," said the professor. "I'll call you later. Now, some men are going to come in here shortly. Try to stay out of sight, but act natural."

With that, the professor ran toward the back of the apartment building. Sure enough, two men dressed in black suits entered the building. They seemed to be looking for someone. The men paid little attention to Adam.

As soon as the men left the lobby, Adam returned to his scooter and rode as quickly as possible. This time he ignored his mom's advice and zipped in and out of the pedestrian traffic. All the while he kept looking over his shoulder to make sure he wasn't being followed by the SUV.

When he arrived back at his apartment, he locked all the doors. He locked all the windows and closed the curtains. The professor had thoroughly spooked Adam. He was sure the mysterious men were going to find him somehow.

Adam pulled out the card and looked at the phone number. He wondered if anything had already happened to the professor. He thought about calling the number right away. Then he thought he'd better wait and see if the professor called him. Adam decided to memorize the number on the card. He might need to eat the card to protect Alfred.

It took a few minutes before Adam remembered the other thing the professor had given him. Adam reached into his pocket and pulled out the object. He recognized what it was. He had one just like it that he used in the computer lab at school. It was a thumb drive, a small computer chip.

It only seemed natural to plug it into a computer and see what happened. Adam had his own laptop computer. He pulled it out of a backpack and turned it on. Adam waited anxiously as the computer went through its start-up routine.

Adam took the opportunity to check out the window. He watched the traffic for several minutes. There was no sign of the black SUV. There was also no sign of Professor Omega.

The little tone in the background told Adam that the computer was ready to be used. He quickly plugged in the thumb drive. A screen popped up asking if he wanted to open the files on the drive. It was the first time that Adam questioned if he should.

Maybe it was some computer virus. His mom would be very mad at him if that were the case. He decided that Alfred wouldn't do that to him. Adam scrolled over the continue button on the screen and clicked the mouse.

A program opened up. A voice came over the computer: "Smile." Adam obeyed the voice and smiled. The computer made a sound like a camera clicking. Adam's smiling face appeared on the screen.

"Frown," said the same voice.

Adam frowned. Again the computer made a camera sound and his frowning face appeared next to his smiling face. A grid of blue lines appeared over the faces. The lines sunk into his eye sockets and popped out around his nose.

The grid broke the faces into small squares. They began to swirl and seemed to drain right into the center of the computer screen. Adam thought it was a cool effect, but there wasn't much of a game to it yet.

Another screen popped up. This appeared to be some kind of form. It asked common questions such as his name, address, height, weight, and age. It also asked some unusual questions such as what do you do best? And what is your greatest weakness?

It wasn't exactly Adam's idea of entertainment. He decided to keep going, not for his sake. He thought the professor might like some feedback about the game. Perhaps that's why the professor gave it to him.

After answering the last question and hitting the enter button on the keyboard, finally a new scene popped up on the computer. Adam had to smile. The scene looked just like his bedroom. The professor must have been inspired by Adam's apartment.

Adam noticed a character sitting at a computer. He started pushing common buttons for moving characters on the computer screen. The arrow buttons generally worked for most games.

The character on the screen rose from the computer. When it turned around to face the door, Adam had to smile. The character looked just like him. Maybe this could be a fun game after all. He could pretend to be in his own little simulated world.

He heard someone enter the apartment. Adam stood up and turned toward the door.

"Adam! Are you home?" said the voice.

"I'm in my room," said Adam. "I'm working on my computer."

"It better be homework and not games," warned his mom from beyond the door.

"It's something for Professor Omega," answered Adam. "I'm giving him a kid's opinion on a project."

"That's nice," said his mom. "But if you have homework, do it first. I'm sure Alfred would understand."

"I have all weekend," said Adam as he moved the simulated Adam forward.

He held the button too long and the character sprung forward. It tripped over a replica of his scooter. In the rush, Adam hadn't put away the real one. He thought it was amazing that the professor could somehow know to put the scooter right in the middle of the floor.

Just then, there was a siren out the window. Adam immediately thought of the professor. He was afraid he might be hurt, or maybe even in some kind of trouble with the police. Maybe the guys in the black suits were detectives.

Adam hopped up to rush to the window. With the curtains drawn and the lights out, the bedroom was very dark. Adam didn't see the scooter until it was too late. He tumbled and fell just like his simulated character in the video game.

"Whoa, now that's amazing," said Adam as he stared back at his feet while lying on the floor.

## Chapter 3
## The Phone Call

"I'm all right," said Adam when his mom knocked on the door.

"That's good to know," said his mom, "But you have a phone call."

"I'm kind of busy now, can you take a message?" asked Adam.

"Am I your personal secretary now?" she said to Adam. "Can he call you back, Alfred?" his mom spoke into the phone.

"Wait!" shouted Adam as he flung open his door. "I'll take it."

When Alfred got on the phone, he was obviously winded. Adam could hear the fear in his voice. The professor had to have been on the run since they last met. Adam thought this was a good sign. He had managed to escape the men in the SUV.

"Did you find the thumb drive?" panted Alfred.

"Yes," said Adam. "And I memorized the phone number."

"That's good," said Alfred. "But the phone number was 515-555-5555. How difficult was …never mind. Now, I'm not sure who I can trust. Don't call the number unless you haven't heard from me in 24 hours. Don't use your home phone and don't tell anyone your name. There's something very important you have to promise me."

"Sure," said Adam.

"Whatever you do," said the professor, "This is important now. DO NOT under any circumstances open the file on the thumb drive."

Adam was silent.

"Do you hear me?" repeated the professor. "Promise me. It's for your own safety."

"Uh oh," sighed Adam into the phone.

"You didn't?" asked the professor.

"I did," answered Adam. "It's not that fun of a game, but it does have potential. I'll take notes."

"Oh, Adam," sighed the professor. He seemed to be lost for words. "Okay, you didn't know better. There's something very important. You cannot stop in the middle of a level. Finish the first level and then exit without storing the file. You'll need to do your homework. I think you should be safe, then."

"Okay," said Adam. "But what about you? Are you safe? Should we call the police or something?"

"I'll be fine. Just don't stop in the middle of the level. Isosceles…"

Adam heard tires screeching to a halt in the distance behind the professor. He heard men shouting in the background and rapidly approaching footsteps. There was a loud painful shout. Then there was the sound of the phone hitting the pavement.

Adam strained to hear what was happening. There seemed to be a struggle of some sort. A second later a strange voice spoke into the phone. The deep voice asked in an angry tone, "Who is this?"

Adam quickly hung up.

He went back to the computer. There was a red dot flashing on the screen. Adam maneuvered his character toward the red dot. It stopped at the bookshelf in his simulated bedroom. The character picked up a book.

It seemed only natural for Adam to maneuver the character toward his desk and sit down. He read the title of the book. It was his math book. The character took out a piece of paper. It began to copy problems from today's assignment.

He peered over the character's shoulder on the screen. Adam hoped to see the products of the multiplication problems the character was working. He figured it wouldn't be cheating to copy off himself. It would be a lot easier too.

No matter how he changed the viewing angle, Adam couldn't see the paper. He made a note of the fact for the professor. The game would be much better and more helpful if he could know all the answers in advance. Maybe, he could even fast forward to see the paper after it was graded so he could correct the mistakes ahead of time. Now Adam was getting excited about the potential of the game. He really wanted to keep playing.

The Adam character on the screen finished his math homework. A box appeared on the computer screen. Enter clue _ _ 9 _. Adam didn't know what to do, and then he realized the awful truth. He would have to do his math homework to find the clue. That must have been what the professor meant by telling him he would need to do his homework.

Adam sighed and got up from the desk. He walked to his bookshelf and picked up the math book. He walked back to his desk and began to solve the problems for his math homework. Sure enough, the only problem that had a nine in the tens place of the product was the last one, 15 times 313.

"I should have known," sighed Adam to himself, "All that extra work for nothing."

Then he realized he would have needed to do it anyway for school on Monday. But that was three days away. He never had it done this early. He was afraid to admit to himself that it actually felt good to not have to keep reminding himself it needed to be done.

With the math homework done, Adam turned his attention back to the game. He now knew the answer for the clue. He typed in 4695. The box went away. Up popped another box.

This box read "Level 1 Complete" and asked for options: store and quit, quit without storing, continue. Adam moused over the choices. He knew what the professor wanted him to do. Adam didn't really want to be disobedient. He knew the professor was trying to protect him.

Adam's fear was that protection from the professor might put the professor in great danger. Maybe Adam could help or at least get enough information to give to the police. As he thought about the choices and possible ramifications he noticed something on the screen.

The scene in the background was no longer his bedroom. Instead it was Professor Omega's apartment. The first thing he noticed was Isosceles jumping at the screen. She kept flopping against it.

Then the door opened. Adam hoped he would see the professor home safe and sound. Instead it was two men in black suits. They began turning things over in the apartment. They were making a huge mess. The men in the black suits were obviously looking for something.

## Chapter 4
## Take It To Another Level

"Sorry Professor," Adam said out loud as he made his choice. "One more level."

He clicked on continue. The box went away. Now, the screen was split. On one side his character was still in his bedroom. On the left side of the computer screen was the scene in the professor's apartment. It looked normal again. The men in suits hadn't been there yet. The one thing that hadn't changed was Isosceles. She was still jumping at the screen.

Adam began to maneuver his character toward the professor's apartment. He moved out the door to the hallway of the apartment building and moved down the steps. The character stopped at the professor's door. Adam tried to move the character forward, but nothing happened. It wouldn't open the door.

Then he realized what he needed to do. Adam took the character back to his own kitchen. The professor had given them a key to his apartment. If he was out of town, Adam would use it to go inside and feed Isosceles.

Adam was amazed at all the details the game knew. Then again, the professor knew the key was in their kitchen hanging on a hook. Once the character got the key, he once again went to the apartment.

This time the character was able to open the door. It stopped at the alarm pad. It asked for an alarm code. Adam wouldn't need to work math problems to find this one. He already knew it. Adam punched in the numbers.

The character walked by the professor's computer. Adam noticed the strange screen saver. The same clip played over and over. It was Isosceles jumping at the screen. There was no other sign of the cat in the simulated apartment.

Adam wondered if Isosceles had gotten out when the professor left, but he wasn't exploring the apartment for the cat. He was looking for whatever the men in suits would be coming for.

Then Adam heard banging on the door. The men in the black suits were trying to break down the door. Adam maneuvered his character to find a hiding place. He went into the professor's bedroom. The screen split again so he could see both the bedroom and the living room.

Adam tried to squeeze the character under the bed. It must have had a solid platform because the character wouldn't go. The only other hiding place was the closet. It seemed the obvious place for the men in suits to look, but he really didn't have much choice.

The men in the black suits crashed into the apartment as Adam's character shook nervously in the closet. Adam thought that was a pretty realistic effect. Just like the time before Adam selected the next level, the men began to tear through the apartment.

Then one of the men in suits picked a clock off the wall. That's when Adam noticed the time. It was seven minutes from now.

"Oh, no!" cried Adam. He wished he could see what happened next. It would have been good to know if the men found him or not. There just wasn't time. He had to find the next clue before them.

Adam raced from his apartment and ran down stairs. He sighed when he reached the door. He had forgotten the key. Adam ran back up the stairs and grabbed it from the hook in the kitchen.

He quickly unlocked the door and went right to the alarm keypad. He hurriedly punched in the code. Then he had another thought. He hit a red button. Adam dead bolted the lock on the door.

As Adam walked by the professor's computer, he once again noted the strange screen saver. It was Isosceles jumping against the screen. Suddenly, someone started jiggling the doorknob. Adam knew it wasn't the professor.

He ran to the bedroom. He lightly kicked beneath the bed. Sure enough, it was solid. The closet was the only place to hide. He had no time to waste as the front door crashed open. The men in black suits were in the apartment and they were starting to turn things over.

Adam hid in the closet. How he wished he could have watched the game a little bit longer. He didn't know what happened next. After a few minutes, the bedroom door opened. Adam could hear the two men in the black suits.

He covered himself up as well as he could while standing between the professor's shirts. He gripped the clothes rod and pulled his feet up so they wouldn't show. Adam wished he was better at pull-ups. He knew he couldn't hold this position for long.

The men weren't searching the bedroom. Instead, they opened the bedroom window and climbed out on the fire escape. Adam heard two more voices behind them.

"It looks like they went out the back," said a policeman.

"There they are, running down the fire escape," said another officer.

Adam listened as the two policemen climbed out the window and followed. Adam sighed in relief as the apartment once again became silent. His last minute thought had worked. Adam had pushed the silent alarm button on the security key pad. He had alerted the police of a break-in.

For the first time he had time to think where the professor might have hidden whatever the men were looking for. As Adam's feet hit the floor of the closet once again, the noticed how organized it was. It reminded him of his own closet after Alfred had helped him rearrange it after the incident with Isosceles and the two dogs.

The professor had been perplexed that Adam left his money lying around.

"What if someone broke in?" asked the professor. "Cash is the one thing they would never pass up. You need a clever hiding place to keep valuables until you need them."

"If I hide it, I might not be able to find it," answered Adam. "At least that's the way it has happened in the past."

"Okay," said the professor as he looked around the room. "This is what I would do. We've already arranged the shoes in your closet. The ones you wear the least are in the back. The ones you wear the most are in the front."

The professor rolled up the cash and pushed it into one of the shoes Adam wore the least.

"Now, if you forget where you hid it, you can at least ask me," said Alfred.

Adam smiled at the memory. The professor had told him the best place to hide something valuable. Sure enough, the shoes were organized from the most worn to the least worn. Adam picked up the shoes from the very back corner of the closet.

## Chapter 5
## Saving Isosceles

Adam shook the shoe. He was right; indeed, something was stored in it. It was a key ring. He picked it up and left the professor's apartment. Adam went right back to the computer in his room.

When he got back, he was surprised at the display on the screen. His character was already standing at the simulated desk waiting for him. Adam stood by his chair and moved the mouse to make the character sit down.

The character typed something on the simulated computer. A box popped up on Adam's screen. He sat down at the desk and read the box. All it said was "enter clue words" and blanks: _ _ _ _ _ g _ _   _ _ _ _ _ _ g _. Adam had no idea what the clue could be, but then he noticed the character on the screen reaching into his pocket.

Adam also reached into his pocket and pulled out the key chain. It had a single key on it. Adam recognized it as a padlock key. There were no words on the key chain. The professor had drawn something on it with a permanent marker. It was a triangle. One side was shorter than the other two.

The math textbook was still on Adam's desk. He picked it up and found the section on geometry. It was just as Adam had suspected. It was a specific kind of triangle. It had two equal sides. That made it an isosceles triangle.

Adam started to type in the letters to complete the clue. He came to the first g before he realized it wasn't going to work. Adam backspaced to the beginning to erase the letters. After looking at the two *g*'s more carefully, Adam decided the first word was *triangle*.

He studied the key chain, trying to get a clue. He was deep in thought when his mom knocked on the door.

"I'm going to the basement to get some files from storage. I'll be right back." She noticed the open math book. "You're really doing your math homework on a Friday? I'm proud of you. Keep up the good work. When you get done, why don't you go see if Jesse can play basketball or something? I don't want you in front of the computer all the time."

"I'm kind of in the middle of something," Adam started to explain, but he didn't want to have to explain anything to her and get her worried about Alfred. "Uh, that might be a good idea. A game of basketball might be fun."

As she left, Adam once again turned his attention to finding the second key word. He was just in the middle of collecting his thoughts when his mother came in again.

"Have you seen the key to Alfred's apartment? I noticed it was missing when I got the key to the storage unit in the basement."

"Oh," said Adam. "I took it. The professor asked me to check on Isosceles."

"Is that what the phone call was about?" asked his mother.

"He did talk to me about Isosceles," said Adam trying to avoid a lie. That was the last word the professor spoke to him after all.

His mother again left the room. Adam picked up the key ring he had found in Professor Omega's seldom used shoe. There had to be more to the clue. Adam was near frustration when his mother interrupted him once more.

"Did you have a bag of toys you wanted to put into the storage unit? I can take them down for you," she asked.

Adam got up and went to his closet. He picked up the bag and brought it to his mom. He was almost irritated by now with all the interruptions, but he didn't want to explain his mood to his mom, and he didn't want to hurt her feelings, so he thanked her as she left.

He stared at the computer screen. The Adam character slapped himself on the forehead.

"Storage, storage, storage," Adam mumbled. "How can I concentrate with all this talk about the storage unit?"

Then it hit him. The second clue word was "storage". Adam slapped his forehead as he thought of how the clue was right before him. Triangle Storage was a place people could store extra stuff. Their apartment had storage units in the basement, but they weren't very large. If anyone needed more space, there was a storage company down the street. It was called Triangle Storage because of the shape of the building.

Adam looked at the box on the screen. He counted the letters. The clue words worked. In the background, Isosceles was still jumping at the screen. He typed in the words Triangle Storage.

Suddenly, a red laser beam shot right out of the screen. Adam dove to the floor in surprise. He quickly realized that if the beam had been aimed at him, he never would have stood a chance. There was no way he could dive faster than a laser beam.

His eyes followed the beam from his computer screen to the ending point. It was right on his bed. A puddle of light began to take shape and turn from red to blue. Adam had to squint at the brightness.

When the beam stopped, Isosceles was sitting on Adam's bed. He thought of the clue words, "Triangle Storage." The cat's name was the same as the term for a triangle with two or more equal sides. The computer had stored the cat.

Adam thought back to the professor's last words on the phone call, "Just don't stop in the middle of the level. Isosceles…"

"So that's what happens if you stop before completing a level," said Adam as he petted the cat. "You get saved into the computer."

Adam looked at the computer screen, "Oh, no!" he shouted.

On the screen was a box that read, "Level 2 complete." It gave him the choice to exit or continue, but it also said "will begin Level 3 in 4 seconds, 3, 2, 1…"

## Chapter 6
## A Piece of Pi

The screen on the computer monitor split into two scenes again. The Adam character was at his desk. The other scene was in front of the Triangle Storage building. Somehow, Adam suspected that a trip to the storage facility was in his future. He picked up the key and put it in his pocket.

He pushed the arrows on the keyboard and the simulated Adam stood up and walked from the bedroom. Adam tried to guide the character out the door. Instead, it stopped and turned toward the kitchen.

"Okay," said Adam. "We'll go into the kitchen."

The character went to the refrigerator and pulled out a square pan. Adam recognized it. His mom had made a special treat for the professor in the pan. She was planning on giving it to him today.

It was meant to be a delicious joke about the formula for the area of a circle. One night the professor was over for dinner. Adam's mom had made a pie for dessert.

"A round pie?" asked the professor. "I thought pie are squared."

Mom laughed, but Adam looked confused. "Every pie I've ever seen was round," said Adam.

"It's a joke," explained his mom. "To find the area of a circle, multiply the radius times the radius and pi. The number that represents pi is 22 divided by 7. R stands for the radius and when we multiply it times itself we say it's squared."

"It's the ratio of any circle's circumference to its diameter in the Euclidean plane," explained the professor.

"Oh, that clears it up," sighed Adam. "Does the number for pi change if it's an apple pie, pumpkin pie, or chocolate cream pie?"

The professor laughed, "No, it's still 3.14285714255714. That's rounded off to the nearest 100 trillionth decimal place, of course."

"It's too complicated for me," said Adam.

"Just round off to the nearest hundredth, then," said the professor. "Pi = 3.14"

*******

Adam turned his thoughts back to the computer screen. The character was now standing by the front door. Adam realized that the square pie had to be a clue. The character was now ready to leave the apartment. Adam guided him toward the elevator.

The door on the elevator opened. A character on the elevator stepped out bouncing a basketball. Adam's character stopped and seemed to be talking to the boy with the ball. Next, it got on the elevator.

Adam guided the character out the door and down the street. It stopped in front of the Triangle Storage building. A box popped up on the screen. It looked like a number keypad. Words were under the keypad: Product = Security Code.

For the second time today, Adam was glad he did his homework. He remembered the number he had to punch in during the first level of the game. He clicked on the numbers 4, 6, 9, and 5. The door to the storage facility opened.

The character entered the building. It started down a hallway and stopped at a sign that directed it toward different numbered hallways. It was a strange sign. One hallway was named breads, the other was named cookies, the next hallway was named pies, and the last hallway was named cakes. It was a strange way to name hallways in a building until he remembered it used to be a bakery.

Adam was glad he knew the clue from the kitchen. He even had a good idea which unit number to go to. He started down the pie hallway. It was lined with what looked like narrow garage doors. Adam stopped in front of the unit numbered 314. The character reached into its pocket and pulled out the key. It placed it in the lock and started to turn it. Suddenly, the character froze on the screen.

No matter what Adam did on the keyboard, the character no longer responded. Adam wasn't sure what that meant. Was there just some problem with his computer or maybe the software? Was the character trying to tell him something? If Adam went to the storage locker was something going to happen to him?

Just when Adam was getting comfortable with the future, this had to happen. Adam reminded himself that he hadn't seen any of the men in black suits. There was no sign that he had been followed.

"The men in the black suits don't even suspect that I know the professor at all. How would they know he was in trouble?" said Adam.

"Meow," answered Isosceles from the corner of the room. She had just snuggled down for a nap. It must have been tiring to jump at the screen all those hours.

Adam got up from the computer and walked out his bedroom door. Just as he reached the front door, Adam stopped. He wondered if there really was a square pie in the refrigerator. He went into the kitchen and opened the refrigerator. Sure enough, it was right there, a chocolate cream square pie. His mom had even made the number 3.14 on the top with chocolate chips.

Adam went into the hallway and waited by the elevator. He would have been worried that his mom might step off and stop him, but he had a good idea what was about to happen. Jessie would be stepping off with a basketball in his hand.

Adam knew what he would say. That was one of the nice things about knowing the future. It gave you a chance to plan ahead. Adam would hand Jessie a note. Adam would ask Jessie to give it to Adam's mom if he didn't return in thirty minutes.

The elevator stopped. Sure enough, Jessie came out, bouncing a basketball. Adam gave him his instructions and Jessie agreed to help. Adam didn't want to get his mom involved if she didn't need to be. He figured he could get to the storage unit and back easily in thirty minutes. He was still uneasy that the character on the screen froze. He might just need his mother's help.

## Chapter 7
## Saving Adam

The elevator stopped at the lobby of the apartment building. Adam stepped off. The door to the elevator closed again and continued down to the basement. With the files she was looking for in her hands Adam's mom waited patiently for the doors to open.

She stepped on the elevator and pushed the button for the sixth floor. She felt a little bump as the elevator started moving. That didn't last for long. It stopped again on the first floor to let on another passenger.

"Good afternoon, Mrs. Lansing. Would you like me to hold one of those bags for you?" Adam's mother offered the older woman as she tucked the folder under her arm.

"That would be so helpful, Patty," said the woman. "I'd set them down, but I have a hard time bending over to pick them up. Plus, they tend to tip over and spill my groceries all over the floor."

Adam's mother smiled as she grabbed the heaviest bag.

"Looks like I got the better end of that deal," said the woman as they rode on the elevator. "I got the bread and you got the canned goods."

"I don't mind," smiled Patty.

"You are such a dear," said Mrs. Lansing. "I just don't know what your husband was thinking when he left you."

The thought made Adam's mom wince at the painful memory. She didn't know if she would ever see her husband again. She wondered if she would ever know what happened. The elevator ride suddenly became quiet as it stopped on the sixth floor.

The two women stepped into the hallway. Mrs. Lansing's apartment was the first on the left. Patty waited for the woman to unlock and open her door. Patty handed her the bag of groceries and continued down the hallway.

She suddenly wanted to give Adam a hug. She wanted to tell him everything would be all right. They would get by somehow and things would get better. Adam's mom walked to his bedroom door and knocked softly. The sound woke Isosceles from her cat nap and she meowed.

“Meow?” repeated Patty. “Are you in there, Adam?”

She opened the door. Isosceles raised her head and squinted as the light from the other room flooded in. She meowed again. Adam’s mom looked around the room and noticed the laptop computer.

“I’m glad he decided to play basketball with Jessie,” she said to herself as she walked to his desk. “But what are you doing here Isosceles?”

She leaned over and looked at the screen. It was the final scene from the storage unit. The character just stood before the unit. She shook her head. Adam knew better to go off and play and leave his computer on. She hit the escape key.

Up popped a box that gave two choices. Adam’s mother thought for a second. She could almost hear him complaining already if she closed his game without saving the settings. She moused over the store and close choice and clicked.

*****

At the storage facility Adam was pleased that the 4695 code got him in the door. He hardly had to look at the sign. He already knew he would travel down the Pie hallway. He was getting a little nervous as he reached unit 314. He smiled a bit as he saw someone had drawn a dot between the 3 and the 1 so it looked like 3.14.

Adam reached into his pocket, pulled out the key. He put it in the lock, but never turned it. Suddenly, Adam was gone. Nevertheless, the hallway was not empty.

*****

There was a knock on the apartment door. Adam’s mom thought it must be Mrs. Lansing. She thought at first to ignore it. She didn’t need the woman to bring up more painful memories. Then she thought again. The woman meant her no harm. Mrs. Lansing just didn’t realize how painful her words had been.

“Hi, can I speak to Adam?” said the child as she answered the door.

“I thought you were playing basketball in the courtyard,” said Adam’s mom.

“I came up for a snack a half-hour ago,” said Jessie. “Is Adam here?”

Adam’s mom was a little concerned, “Jessie, wasn’t Adam with you? Is he all right?”

“No,” said Jessie. “I saw him get on the elevator.”

The boy pulled out a piece of paper from his pocket. He handed it to Adam’s mom. “He asked me to give you this if he wasn’t back in a half hour.”

Adam’s mom glanced at the note. It only had two words and numbers written on it. She recognized Adam’s handwriting easily enough.

"Did he say anything else to you?" she asked.

"He just told me to give you this note if he wasn't back in thirty minutes," said Jessie. "Is he all right?"

Adam's mom stepped past him into the hallway. She ran toward down the steps, not wanting to wait for the elevator that could sometimes be slow moving.

"Should I call the police?" Jessie yelled after her.

Adam's mom stopped and tried to act calm, "No, don't do that. I'm sure Adam is all right."

She wasn't that convincing, but Jessie figured she was an adult. She knew what she was doing. He turned and walked back toward his apartment. Just as he reached the door, he noticed the elevator stopping.

Two men in dark suits stepped out. One of them stopped and looked at Jessie carefully.

"That's not him," said the other as they continued down the hallway.

Jessie stepped into his apartment and locked the door behind him.

Adam's mother reached the Triangle Storage building. She quickly punched in the four digit code. She couldn't help but run down to the Pie hallway. Her heart sank when she saw it was empty. She quickly checked the Bread, Cookie, and Cake hallways. No one was in any of them.

She returned to the Pie hallway and stopped at unit 314. It was the last one in the hall. The padlock was off the door. That puzzled her. She looked around again for Adam. There was still no sign of her son.

She pulled out her cell phone and punched in a number. The sound of a motor could be heard above her. A wall slid from the ceiling and concealed the last storage unit from all the others. She lifted the garage-style door on the unit. Behind it was a solid steel wall.

Adam's mom placed her hand on the wall. A blue glow appeared around her hand. A door opened out of nowhere in the wall and Adam's mom stepped through.

## Chapter 8
## Not Just a Twin

Adam found himself standing back in his own room. There was something different about it. Everything seemed less real. It was almost like a dream. Then he turned around and saw the paw prints.

They were suspended in the middle of the air. As Adam reached out to touch them his hand was stopped. It was like there was a window of some sort, but he couldn't see any glass. He pressed both hands up to the surface and pushed.

It was an invisible wall of some sort. Adam started to panic. He backed up and started to make a run at the barrier. Right before he sprang into action he heard a loud groan behind him.

Adam turned around. There lying on the floor was a boy bent over and rubbing his shoulder. Adam couldn't see his face, but the boy was in obvious pain. Adam decided not to charge at the wall after all. He wanted to learn from the other boy's mistake.

Suddenly, the boy sprang up. "Thanks for changing your mind. You don't know the pain you spared us."

Adam was shocked at what he saw. Before him stood his identical twin brother. There was only one problem. He didn't *have* an identical twin brother. In fact, he was an only child.

"Don't be mad at me for pretending to be you. I was the only you here until you invaded my world," said the simulated Adam.

"I wasn't thinking that," Adam started to protest. "Wait a second, I just started thinking that."

"I know," said the other Adam. "I'm the future you. You know, the one you've been playing with all afternoon."

"Oh no," sighed the real Adam. "I've been stored in the game."

"Something like that," said the simulated Adam. "Now, don't be like that. You might like it here so much you won't want to leave."

"What do you mean?" asked the real Adam. Then he gasped, "Now I know what you mean. You want to escape here before me. You want to become the real me."

"And I will too," said the simulated Adam as an evil smile spread on his face. "You see, whatever solution you think up I'll know before you. I'm your future. I'll always be at least one step ahead of you."

Adam couldn't hold himself back. He dove for the simulated Adam who simply turned out of the way.

"That was too easy," said his future self.

"That was too easy," the real Adam repeated.

"That's right," said the simulated Adam. "You controlled me since the beginning of the game. Now, I control you. How does it feel…Don't answer I already know how you feel! Now, I have work to do if I want to be real."

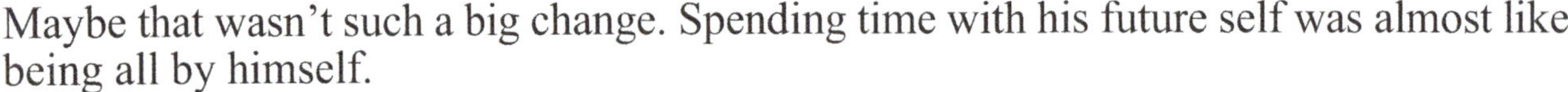

With that the future Adam raced toward a bedroom wall. The real Adam watched as the simulated boy passed right through it. Adam was somewhat relieved to be alone. Maybe that wasn't such a big change. Spending time with his future self was almost like being all by himself.

Adam reached out to the wall the simulated Adam had just passed through. It felt real to him. He pressed against it. It felt as firm as the walls of his real apartment. Adam thought that was strange. Maybe his future self wasn't all that he seemed to be.

He remembered the clues he would get in the video game. Maybe there was a clue left in this simulated room. Adam decided to check out all his secret hiding places. The first of course was the pair of shoes in the back of the closet.

Adams heart sank when he picked them up. Inside was a note. It was written with his handwriting. All it said was, "too late." The future Adam had already searched for any clues.

Then the simulated Isosceles woke from her nap. She rubbed up against Adam's legs to get his attention. Adam reached down to pet her. As he reached out his hand, the cat bolted for the computer on the desk.

He just had to shake his head as he looked at the screen. He was looking at a simulated computer with a simulated version of the game on it. When he looked closely, he could see another simulated screen on the computer in the simulated room. It was like those department store mirrors that showed three sides at once. The reflections seemed to go on forever.

Up popped a box on the computer screen. It read, "He only knows your thoughts when you're in the same room." Adam thought that was strange. It was more of a message than a clue. Someone was speaking to him.

Adam typed back, "Who is this?"

"Professor Omega," came the answer.

The professor! Adam was relieved that the professor was all right. This was good news. If anyone could get him out of here, the professor could.

"How do I get out of here?" typed Adam.

"Don't obey your mother," came the answer.

Now, that was more of a clue than a message, thought Adam. Why couldn't the professor be clearer? Adam sighed. This was the professor he was thinking about. Nothing was ever too clear with the professor.

Adam remembered all the times he asked the professor about his past. He was always given some kind of vague answer or something that didn't quite make sense. It was almost as if the professor didn't know the answers himself.

"What do you mean?" Adam typed.

"CPU= name."

"I'm still confused," Adam typed.

Suddenly the computer screen went black.

## Chapter 9
## Secret Agent Mom

The storage unit was completely empty. It was only about five feet deep and six feet wide. The steel door closed behind Adam's mom. She turned around and faced the small screen on the front wall. She leaned into the screen.

A copy of her eye appeared on the screen. A grid of blue lines broke the image down into pieces. The words "Access Approved" popped up on the screen. Then a number keyboard touchscreen took its place.

Adam's mom punched in eight numbers. The whole storage unit plunged through the floor when Adam's mom touched the enter key. Somewhere deep under the city, the elevator stopped. The door opened.

Patty hesitated. She hadn't stepped foot in the room since she had searched it for her husband the night he didn't return home. It looked just the same. The rows of LED lights give it that familiar glow. She sighed at the memory.

She walked down the narrow rows toward her office in the back corner. It was dark when she opened the door. She sat down at the desk and flipped on her computer. Patty planned to pull up the video footage from the security cameras at Triangle Storage.

Maybe it would give her clue to Adam's disappearance. She waited anxiously as the computer came back to life after being asleep so many months. Patty typed in her passcodes. Next, she went to video archive and guessed at the time Adam would have been there.

Sure enough, she saw him walk down the hallway. He was looking all around, as if he was worried about something. Adam's mom watched as he pulled the key from his pocket and placed it in the lock. Then it happened. Adam vanished.

Patty shook her head. Was she missing something? She rewound the video and played it back more slowly. The same thing happened. Adam was there and then he wasn't. She was beginning to wonder if someone had hacked into the video and erased what happened next. Then she watched the time stamp. That was the set of numbers on the video that showed when it was filmed.

No time seemed to be missing. It would have taken a real expert to fake the video on such short notice. Patty wasn't even sure it was possible, especially to fool a trained eye like hers.

She buried her face into her hands and began to cry. When she looked up again, she caught just the very end of something else on the video. The garage-like door was closing on storage unit 314. She just caught a glimpse of the fingers pulling the door down from the inside.

A chill ran down her spine. Someone else was in the underground computer lab. She peered through the window and slowly rose from her desk. Patty locked the door and sat back down.

She kept glancing between her computer screen and the window in her office. She didn't see anyone. The video replayed showing Adam vanish once again. A few seconds later, another person appeared. Patty leaned into the screen to get a closer look.

From the angle of the camera, she couldn't see a face. Then suddenly the person glanced around quickly. Could it be? Patty quickly backed the footage up again. This time she was able to freeze it at the precise moment.

She gasped. It was the professor. When she looked up she gasped again. Professor Omega was standing right outside her office. He seemed as surprised as she was. He was trying to come in, but the door was locked.

Patty raced to the window and drew back the curtains. The professor knocked on the door. He was yelling to her to let him in. She leaned against the door in fear wondering how he managed to break in. She also wondered how she could get past him. There seemed to be no other way out of the office.

Then she noticed the air shaft. Being so far underground, the office needed a source for air. If she could get the metal grid off the opening in the wall, she figured she could squeeze through. She remembered the little tool box her husband, Caleb, had put in the back of the filing cabinet in her office. It was to encourage her to stop borrowing his tools.

She quickly dug through it and found a screwdriver. She turned her attention back to the air shaft. In the meantime, the professor had stopped knocking on the door. Patty's nervous, shaking hands made it difficult to take out the screws.

She was even more rushed when she heard the sound of a key in the lock. The door knob turned. In stepped the professor. Patty jumped to her feet and gripped the screwdriver tightly. She was ready to use it as a weapon if she needed to.

"It's okay, Tressy. I'm here to help," said the professor.

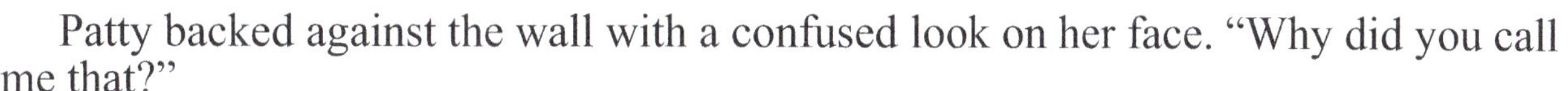

Patty backed against the wall with a confused look on her face. "Why did you call me that?"

"What?" asked the professor.

"You called me Tressy. The only person who ever called me that was my husband," she explained. "He didn't even call me that it public, only when we were alone. It was our secret name."

"I'm sorry," said the professor. "I don't know why I said it. I've been thinking strange thoughts lately. It's like memories, but in some ways it seems like they happened to someone else. I really can't explain it. But please know, I'm not a threat to you. I'd never do anything to hurt you or Adam."

"What do you know about Adam?" demanded Patty. "Where is he? Where did you take him?"

The professor sighed. "I didn't take him, but I know where he is."

He turned and walked to another part of the underground computer lab. Patty quickly realized he was leading her to her husband's office. Inside, the computer was up and running.

"How did you do this? Who do you work for?" asked Patty. "There's no way you could have gotten past all our security measures by yourself. Who helped you?"

"Believe it or not, nobody," said the professor. "I didn't even use any high tech equipment. The best way I can explain it is to say I just did what came natural to me."

"No, no, no," said Patty. "Even if you made a one in a billion guess at the passwords and access codes, there's still the hand scanner and the eye scanner. You couldn't have guessed at that. You had to get access to the system. Tell me once and for all who you are working for."

"Well," said the professor. "Up until a few days ago, I thought I was working for the government. When I discovered this place, something didn't add up. If I was working for the government, why didn't they know about this lab?

"Then who are you working for?" asked Patty again. "How did you get past the hand and eye screen?"

"Tressy, I just don't know. This morning I noticed two men in dark suits watching me at the coffee shop. I've been running from them all day. They almost caught me this afternoon while I was on the phone with Adam. Fortunately, I've been working on a new invention. It's called a stun glove. It would cause a normal man to collapse and roll around on the ground."

"Did something different happened with the men in suits?" asked Patty.

"They lit up like a blue neon sign," explained the professor as he waved his hands to show how big the glow was.

That's when Patty noticed the scar. It's a wonder she had never seen it before. Then again, it was a small scar and not easily noticed. It was the exact size and in the same place as the one on her husband's hand.

She stepped closer and looked into his eyes. Was it possible? He was so much older, at least twenty years older.

"Caleb?" she asked.

The professor shook his head, "I don't know. I can't remember."

## Chapter 10
## Superior Adam

There was a knock at the bedroom door. Adam wasn't going to answer it. The door didn't open. Instead a person stepped right through it. Adam expected to see his simulated self.

Instead, this person was much older. He wore an expensive suit and seemed to be quite pleased with himself. The character circled around Adam. He kept turning to keep his eye on him.

"Why don't you recognize me?" asked the man. Then he laughed. "You got me there. You're exactly right. If I already know what you're thinking why bother asking the question. You were such a bright child. Thanks for giving me such a promising start, but I can take it from here."

Adam tried not to think of anything. His future self had found a way to get even further ahead of him.

"Where did you go?" asked Adam.

"To the big brain, of course," said the simulated adult Adam. "I just took advantage of its processing power and projected us a bit farther into the future. Now I'm not only bigger than you, I'm smarter than you too. I have a good college education and am very successful. You'll never be able to out think me now and escape. Consider me the official new you."

"What's going to happen to me?" asked Adam.

"Don't worry," said the adult Adam. "I'll go clear out some memory for you."

With that, the simulated Adam once again stepped through a wall.

"You won't be able to do that when you're real, you know," Adam yelled after him.

He quickly turned back to the computer. It was still dark. Adam wondered if he had been able to disguise his thoughts well enough. He tried to put any thoughts about the clues the professor had given out of his mind when the future Adam was in the room.

Now he had to remember what the clues were. It quickly came back to him. Don't obey your mother and CPU= name. Adam wondered what they meant. Being around his mother and father, he knew what CPU meant. CPU stood for central processing unit. It was the brains of the computer. Adam couldn't figure out the rest of the equation.

"It's probably better to solve the first clue first," Adam reasoned. "What could it mean to not obey my mother? The professor was always telling him to do the exact opposite. Why did he change his advice all of the sudden?"

Adam thought back to conversations he had with the professor whenever his mother told him to do something like homework, limiting TV or computer games, and eating right.

"You may not appreciate it now, but you want to have a strong future," said the professor. "Obey your mother. She's giving you good advice."

Adam thought for a minute and smiled. He knew just what to do. This might even be fun. He walked to his desk in his simulated bedroom. He picked up the simulated homework and tore it into pieces.

"That's the last homework I'm ever going to do. I'm going to be the dumbest student in school. As soon as I'm old enough, I'll drop out of school. I'll never go to college."

Next, he went to the kitchen. He dumped out all the nutritious food. "I never really liked it anyway," he said.

If it was anything the least bit good for him, he washed it down the garbage disposal. He threw out the vitamins. Next, he made himself a nice big, fatty, sugary snack.

"Welcome to my new diet," said Adam. "From now on I'm only eating candy and ice cream. This is the life for me. While I'm at it I think I'll give up sports and any form of exercise."

He plopped down in front of the television and turned it on. An educational program was on the screen.

"Not for this boy," said Adam. "I need some mindless entertainment. He flipped though the channels until he found a program his mother hated. She said it would only dull his brain.

"Just what the professor ordered," laughed Adam. "I'm going to record this and watch it eight hours a day for the rest of my life. There should be some real long term negative effects in my future now"

Adam was right. His older future self returned once again. This time he didn't look quite so confident. He didn't have the twinkle of confidence in his eye. The future him was several pounds heavier.

He no longer had that look of success about him. The future self had no ambition at all. He didn't care to become real. In fact, the future Adam didn't care much about anything, except eating Adam's ice cream and candy.

He plopped down on the couch next to the real Adam and watched the TV. The sillier the program became, the more the future self laughed. Adam could only hope that his future could be changed when this was all over.

"Look!" said Adam as he pointed out the window at nothing in particular.

The future Adam stood and walked to the window. He stared out the window with a goofy expression on his face. Adam grabbed the bowl of ice cream and hid in under a table. When the future self turned around he began looking around for it.

He stuck out his lip and began to pout, "Where did my ice cream go?"

"I put it away," said Adam.

"Oh," slumped the future Adam. "Where is it?"

"It's in the CPU," said Adam like he was speaking to a two-year old. "If you take me to the CPU, I'll give you back the ice cream."

"Goody, goody!" said the future Adam as he jumped up and down for joy.

Now Adam just hoped he hadn't made the future Adam too dumb to find the CPU. He went to the computer. Adam looked up some information about the central processing unit. He quickly memorized just enough information to make his future self smart enough to find it, but not smart enough to know the reason for going there.

## Chapter 11
## Jessie's Fast Break

Jessie knew something terrible was about to happen in Adam's apartment. He felt bad when he realized he hadn't even shut the door when Adam's mom ran out. The boy had to think fast because he could hear heavy footsteps pass his door.

He unhooked all the chains and unlocked all the locks. Jessie would have to time this just right. He had one piece of information that would help him. The elevator made a slight buzzing sound just before the doors closed.

The boy grabbed his basketball and bounced it down the hall toward the men. They seemed angry to have to deal with him. The taller man gave him a scowl that normally would have frightened a child. It worked. Jessie was frightened enough, he just wasn't about to show it.

"What do you want kid?" asked one of the men.

"The first floor," said the boy.

"This elevator's taken," said the other man.

"We can all ride together," said Jesse. "I'll share."

He eyed the taller man. He was carrying something that looked very familiar. It was Adam's backpack. It wasn't his school backpack. It was the one he kept his computer in for traveling.

"I think I know you," Jessie spoke to the taller man as the elevator door opened. He needed to stall just a few more seconds.

"I don't think so," said the taller man.

Jessie heard the familiar buzzing. "You're a famous basketball player!"

At that Jessie tossed the basketball toward the man's face. He instinctively reached up to catch it to protect his head, dropping the backpack in the process. Jessie caught it and dove between the man's legs and onto the elevator just as the door closed.

The elevator stopped on the fourth floor. The woman with the two dogs that attacked Isosceles was waiting to go down. Jessie saw the men run by on the steps. They were racing him to the bottom floor. Jessie knew if he continued to go down on the elevator, he was going to get caught.

Jessie ran back up the stairs to his apartment. He then realized the men knew where he lived. He looked out the window. The fire escape looked clear. He kept his eyes open for signs of trouble as he went all the way to the courtyard below.

He was glad he was on the basketball team. The coach had trained them to run fast. He zipped down the alley to the street. There were no men in black suits. He walked more calmly and tried to blend in with the crowd on the sidewalk.

Jessie didn't notice the black SUV following him. He had just about reached the Triangle Storage building when they stopped. The two men were on him before he knew what happened. They began to drag him toward the street. Jessie struggled with all his might.

He was afraid he was being kidnapped. "Help! Help!" he started yelling.

People started running toward him. The men in black suits noticed. They yanked the backpack off Jessie's back and let him drop to the sidewalk. The SUV sped away.

After assuring everyone he was all right, Jessie stopped in front of the Triangle Storage building. It was an odd shaped building that was actually shaped like a triangle. Jessie remembered the piece of paper Adam had given him. He punched in the code.

He started looking around the lobby when he heard voices. He hoped it was Adam and his mother. He hid behind some empty boxes stacked near the wall. Jessie did recognize the woman's voice. It was Adam's mother. He peered between the boxes.

Jessie recognized the man with her too. He lived on the fifth floor. Everyone called him the professor. Jessie knew that Adam and he were friends, but with all the strange things going on, he didn't want to give himself away just in case.

The two adults left the building. Jessie decided to follow from a distance. They went back toward the apartment building. Jessie dashed in and out of doorways trying to stay out of sight as he followed.

Adam's mom caught a glimpse of him doing this. She had been looking over her shoulder to make sure there were no men in the black suits. She turned around and started walking toward him. Jessie started running the other way.

"Jessie, get back here," yelled Patty.

Jessie stopped. He knew if the professor meant her any harm, she wouldn't try to involve him also. So he turned and ran toward them. He told them about the men in suits, the SUV, and the stolen computer.

"That's not good," sighed the professor.

"Are you saying what I think you're saying?" asked Patty.

"If they have the computer, they have Adam," he sighed.

They took Jessie back to his apartment and made sure he was safe. Next, they checked out both of their apartments. Both had been broken into. There were no clues.

"We really need to call the police. Maybe they can find fingerprints or some other clue that will help," said Patty.

"They won't," sighed the professor. "I'm pretty sure they didn't leave any finger prints.

## Chapter 12
## Finding the Brain

It took longer than Adam would have liked. You would think riding on beams of electrons would make travel extremely quick. It would be too, unless your guide was as dimwitted and easily distracted as the future Adam.

They rode from circuit board to circuit board looking for the CPU. Adam was nearly exasperated when they landed in a large room that reminded him of a warehouse. The future Adam was fascinated by all of Adam's old video game scores and levels that he had mastered. Adam knew they were in the wrong place.

He wandered around until they came to an opening that looked like a large warehouse door. Adam and Adam wandered into it. The first thing he came to was a set of large numbers, 3.14. Of course, Adam recognized it.

"Pi," he said out loud.

"Oh, good," said the older Adam. "I'm getting hungry."

He took a bite out of the 4. "Yum, apple!"

The real Adam continued looking around. He came to a door and opened it. Inside was a simulation of the professor's apartment. The next door was his apartment. Adam began to realize where he was. He was in the thumb drive. These were all the files from the game the professor had created.

He would have liked to look around more, but really wanted to get to the CPU. Adam decided it was time to leave.

"Let's go," he said to the other Adam.

The older Adam wasn't paying attention. He had his ear to a door and giggled. Adam stopped to watch the strange sight. The future Adam would knock and say the words "restore me". This happened three times in the few seconds Adam watched.

He went over and grabbed his future self's terribly weak and out-of-shape arm. The future self motioned for Adam to join him. He sighed. If he went along with it for a few seconds, maybe the future self would leave.

Adam pressed his ear against the door. What he heard almost made him fall to his knees. A voice cried out from the other side, "Restore me." It wasn't the words that shook him; it was the voice. He knew it. The voice was his father's.

Adam immediately reached for the door knob. It dissolved right in his hands, then it came back. The future Adam smiled and waved a finger in Adam's face.

"Can't open it, yet," he said. "You must play by the rules."

"The rules!" exclaimed Adam. "There are rules? Since when have there been rules in this game?"

"Ask CPU," said the future Adam. "He's very, very, very, very, smart."

"I got it after the first very," sighed Adam. "Are you ready to take me there now?"

The future Adam smiled brightly, "Yep, it's time."

Adam and his future self hopped on the next electron beam and resumed their trip to the CPU. The future Adam had to take the long way there, of course. He stopped and enjoyed the breeze from the cooling fan. He checked all the video and audio inputs for any new entertainment. Finally, they arrived in a room that was filled with swirling lights.

The electron took them right to the center and dropped them off. Adam looked around the room. It was like a clear summer night sky. There must have been billions of lights.

"They're like stars," said Adam.

"They're buttons," said the future Adam. "But not shirt buttons. Don't get confused, like me!"

Adam shook his head. He was not looking forward to the future if that was him in twenty years. Still, his future was right about one thing. Each light was a button, and it wasn't a shirt button. They were each buttons that could be pressed to start something.

"Push the button to leave," said the future Adam.

"Which button?" asked Adam, "There are billions of them."

"Oh," said the future self. "Push the right button."

“You’re a lot of help,” sighed Adam. “Which one is the right button?”

“CPU equals name,” said the future Adam.

“The clue,” said Adam. “That’s right there is a clue. If I can find buttons with the letters A, D, and M, I can spell my name.”

“Our name,” smiled the older Adam. “What color is A?”

“A is not a color, it’s a letter. Do any of the buttons have letters on them?” asked Adam.

“Just colors,” smiled the other Adam.

“Then spelling is not the clue. It has to have something to do with a color.”

“My name!” shouted the other Adam.

“My name?” thought the real Adam.

Suddenly, he remembered a conversation with the professor. They were talking about names. Omega was the last letter of the Greek alphabet. Alpha was like our letter a. Sometimes the letter a was used as a prefix that meant first. Adam was of course the first man. The professor explained the Adam came from the word that meant “to be red.”

That was it. Adam hugged his future self and said, “You’re a genius.”

“We’re a genius,” said the future self.

Adam knew which button to push. It was the first red button. He was surprised as he studied the buttons that there were several blues, greens, yellows, purples, and even oranges. The first red one he saw was at least ten feet above his head. There was nothing to stand on to reach it.

He desperately looked around the room. The only thing around was more buttons. He rested his hand over his eyes and tried to think of something. The next thing he knew, he was floating in the air. Well, he wasn’t exactly floating. His future self was lifting him to his shoulders.

## Chapter 13
## Tracking Adam

"Does Adam still keep his computer in the dark blue backpack with the green trim?" asked the professor.

"Yes," answered Patty.

The professor walked to the book shelf. He scanned the titles and picked up a very thick book. The professor pulled it off the shelf. Patty looked on in amazement when the professor opened it up and pulled out an electronic device."

"It's a GPS," explained the professor.

"Of course," said Patty. "But how did it get there and how did you know where to find it?"

The professor just shrugged his shoulders as he turned it on. "How many backpacks did Adam lose before Caleb decided to put a tracking chip in it?"

"How did you know?" asked Patty again.

"Look, it's only a few blocks from here. Let's go, Tressy, our son needs us," said the professor.

"Caleb, is that you," asked Patty as she stared into his eyes.

"I don't know," answered the professor. "Maybe, I just don't remember clearly. I just know we have to hurry."

The professor and Patty rushed to the street. They ran about four blocks. The professor stopped and looked at the screen on the tracker. He turned to his left and looked down the alley.

"Stay back," he ordered Patty.

He walked slowly between the two buildings. At the end of the alley was a garage door and a smaller door beside it. The professor was still watching the screen. This was the place.

He reached the door knob and turned it slowly. The first thing he saw was the black SUV parked inside the garage. The professor heard voices up the stairs to an office. He climbed them one by one, fearing any creaking sound would give him away.

******

Back at the CPU, the real Adam was balancing himself on the shoulders of the simulated Adam. He stretched as far as he could. Just as real Adam's finger reached the button, the future Adam hiccupped. The real Adam lost his balance as he swayed backward, then forward. With one final push the real Adam made a leap for the button.

******

The professor reached for the doorknob. Suddenly, there was an explosion of blue light in the room. Professor Omega flew across the garage, landed against the SUV, and slumped to the floor.

Patty saw what happened. The door and garage door shattered in the explosion. She raced down the alley and into the building. Under the debris she found the professor. Patty rested his head in her lap and cried.

She looked up at the office. A blue light was still flickering and began to fade. She gasped as she saw the shape of a child.

"Adam?" she cried.

"Mom!" said Adam as he raced down the steps.

He ran toward her, and then slowed down as he saw her lap. There were cuts on the professor's head. He was bleeding, but didn't seem to be in any pain.

"Is the professor alive?" asked Adam as tears began to form.

"Barely," whispered his mom has she stroked the professor's head gently. "And he's not the professor. He's your dad."

"No!" cried Adam. "This can't be happening!"

"Hey Adam," shouted a voice from the office.

Future Adam came out carrying the computer and walked down the stairs. "You're right. I do have to use doors now. I tried and tried to walk through that wall. I'm not so sure I'm going to like being real. Can you restore me?"

Adam took the computer from his future self. His mother looked on in amazement.

"Who is this?" asked his mother.

"Future me," sighed Adam.

"Oh, no," cried his mother. "My poor baby!"

Adam opened the computer. It was still working. In fact, the game was still on the computer. A box popped up. It read, End of Level. Enter command.

"What command?" asked Adam. "I've got to enter something or this craziness will never end."

Future Adam ran and smacked right into the back of the SUV. He was still trying to pass through things. The future Adam sat in the rubble.

"Restore me!" cried future Adam.

"That's it!" said Adam as he typed

A green swirl of light came from the computer. It bathed all of them in light. Patty and Adam closed their eyes to the brightness. A few seconds later it faded.

"Where are we, Tressy?" asked the man in Patty's lap as they opened their eyes.

Adam's mom's face brightened, "Caleb! You're back."

Adam's father was restored to his younger self. He was no longer the professor. The scratches and all signs of injury were gone. He stood to his feet and started shaking off the dust.

Then he looked at Adam. He expected a big, warm, smile from his dad. Instead there was a look of horror on his face. He reached down and ripped the computer from Adam's lap.

"End," said Caleb as he pushed the button and sighed in relief.

Adam looked at the screen. It asked, "Do you want to continue?"

Adam was confident his father chose the best response. He wasn't sure he would ever want to play a video game again. The response box closed.

"Hey look!" said Adam as he turned the screen to his parents.

The men in black suits were bouncing against the computer screen trying to get out. Future Adam was in the background eating candy and watching television. It was the same mindless show Adam had taught him to watch and enjoy.

"I recognize the electro-bots," said Caleb. "They're the ones that aged me before I was able to escape. Who's that goofy character in the background?"

Adam's mom sighed, "That's our son in the future."

"No it's not," said Adam. "I'm going to eat right, study hard, exercise, and do what you tell me to do."

"Will you look at that, Tressy?" Adam's dad smiled proudly as he held the screen up. "It changed right before our eyes."

"I want to see," said Adam.

"You will someday," smiled his mom.

His dad turned off the computer, pulled out the thumb drive, and smashed it to bits under the heel of his shoe.

"In the future," smiled his dad. "In your very bright, future!"

*******

Three weeks later, in an undisclosed Washington, D. C. location…

Report from Agents CE4695 and PE3142 on the termination of project Electro-bot Force.

The file clerk stamped the envelope as "Top Secret", and stuck it in a cardboard box. It was placed in a warehouse with thousands of other brown file boxes in a secret storage facility, never to be seen again.

# The Fountain

by Brian Davis
illustrations by Ron Wheeler

When Micah and Lacey spend a week with their grandfather, they get more than they expected.

It all starts with the discovery of a mysterious fountain

Between alligators and a stranger who claims to be over a hundred years old, the two children are in for quite an adventure.

## Chapter 1
## Lakeland

"I'm not sure having him take care of the kids was such a good idea," said Adel as she watched out the window.

"It will be all right," assured her husband Joe. "Your dad seemed up to it. He will enjoy the company."

"He's lost a step," said Adel. "I was surprised to see him use the cane."

"Just in the morning, until his joints loosen up," Joe repeated his father-in-law's explanation.

"I wish he'd take us up on the offer and come live with us. I worry so much about him," said Adel.

Adel watched her father slowly walk to the old tractor. Adel's two children hopped in a wagon that was attached behind it. The tractor was the same one she had used to cut the grass when she was a teenager. The little red tractor seemed old then. Now it seemed ancient.

"We'll be out of the country for two weeks!" said Adel. "What would they do if something happened?"

"Daryl is down the road. He's an EMT. Help is only a minute away. That's better than back home in the Atlanta. The kids programmed his number into their phones. They also know to call 911. And if we needed to, my company can fly us back in a matter of hours. They're as safe here as anywhere we could leave them. They're even safer here than if we took them with us."

"We haven't been back here in so long," said Adel. "I hadn't realized dad had grown so…frail."

"He's been by himself since your mom died three years ago. He's perfectly capable of watching over our two little angels," smiled Joe.

"They better be on their best behavior for him. I don't want dad to be stressed."

"I think you made that clear to them on the drive here," replied Joe. "You brought it up about every fifteen minutes. You do realize we have two pretty good kids, don't you?"

"Yes," sighed Adel. "But they can still be demanding. It's not easy raising two kids, even when they do behave most of the time."

Lacey and Micah jostled as they rode in the back of the wagon. The old tractor pulled them down a path between large bald cypress trees. They kept their eyes peeled for alligators. They hoped they would get to see one. The children had heard stories about their grandfather wrestling them when he was younger.

The lake was on their left. Cypress trees grew up in the water. Micah and Lacey had never seen trees like them. They look like the roots were growing above the water. They had small balls growing on them. The leaves reminded them of green feathers.

The tractor coasted to a stop. Grandpa turned off the engine. It gave a couple of loud pops as it shut down. The sound made Micah smile. He was sure if there were alligators around, they now knew that people were in the area.

Grandpa walked ahead of the tractor. He stared off into the distance. Lacey and Micah joined him. Micah pulled back a branch to see what his grandfather was staring at.

It was a large, flat-bed semi-truck. It seemed out of place by the lake. In the back of the truck was a machine.

"What is it?" asked Lacey.

"It's a tree cutter," said Grandpa. "They'll bring in bulldozers after they clear the trees."

"Why would they do that?" asked Micah.

"They're going to build houses," said Grandpa sadly.

"Why are you letting them do that?" asked Micah.

"I'm not letting them," sighed Grandpa. "I have no choice. I don't own that land. My property stops here. They tried to buy me out too."

"Who would want to build a house in a lake?" asked Lacey.

"There won't be a lake," answered Grandpa. They'll drain it and fill it in with dirt."

"But you'll still have your lake, right?" asked Lacey.

Grandpa stared down at the ground. He kicked at the dirt. "No, it's all one lake. When they drain it, my part will be gone too."

"That's not right," said Micah. "They're stealing your lake. How can they get away with it?"

"They got it approved with the county commission," said Grandpa. "I fought them for months."

"Did you punch them?" asked Lacey.

"No," said Grandpa. "I felt like it a few times, but that's not how adults solve problems. I used laws to try to protect my land."

"So they're breaking the law?" asked Micah as he pointed at the truck.

"They had one idea of what the law said. I had another," sighed Grandpa. "Sometimes it has to do with who has the most influence."

"What's influence?" asked Lacey.

"In this case," answered Grandpa. "It's money."

Grandpa turned around and slowly walked back to the tractor. Lacey and Micah followed. They hopped in back of the wagon and watched their grandfather slowly climb up to the tractor's seat.

Sound echoed off the lake as the tractor puttered back toward the house. Grandpa turned around and pointed toward the bank of the lake. Lacey and Micah looked. An alligator turned and slipped back into the water. It was only about three feet long.

The children made sure their hands and feet were tucked into the wagon. They remembered the instructions their grandfather had given them. He told them to keep any body parts they liked away from the gators.

Soon they were back at the house. Adel was standing on the porch. She seemed anxious when the children first caught sight of their mother. A relieved smile broke out on her face.

Their father came outside too. He carried a pitcher of cool lemonade and some glasses. The kids hopped off the wagon and ran to the porch as soon as the tractor stopped. They were halfway through their first glass before Grandpa reached the porch.

"Is there still a lake?" Adel asked her father.

"Today there is," said Grandpa. "I wouldn't count on it being there tomorrow. They brought in the equipment to clear the trees."

"I'm sorry Dad. I know what this means to you," said Adel. "Maybe it's time to move on from here. There are nice retirement communities near our house. It might be a good change for you. I'd love to be able to spend more time with you."

Grandpa sighed heavily, "You may be right. I'm not getting any younger. There was a time where I would have had a lot more fight in me. Ten years ago, nobody would get away with draining my lake."

## Chapter 2
## Gator Wranglers

Lacey and Micah watched out of the upstairs window as the truck came up the driveway. The tires kicked up dust from the gravel road. They ran down to the front porch. Grandpa was blocking the way.

"Can't we come out yet?" complained Micah.

"What do you think your mother would say?" asked Grandpa.

"She left two days ago. You're in charge now," Micah encouraged his grandfather.

"Yes," said Grandpa. "And, in this case, I think she would be right to be so protective. The gators are pretty stirred up. I don't blame them for wanting to take a bite out of someone. Still, I don't want to see that happen to anyone, especially you two."

Both Lacey and Micah lowered their heads in sadness. They hadn't been outside the last two days. They expected that to change when the truck arrived. The white truck had the words "Gator Grabbers" painted on the sides.

"Are they going to kill the gators?" asked Lacey.

"Oh heavens no!" exclaimed her grandfather. "I wouldn't have any part of that. They'll be relocated to a wildlife preserve. As long as they don't become a nuisance, nobody should harm them. I'm sure they'll be happier living there than in the middle of a housing addition. Maybe I can get the gator grabbers to toss me onto that truck too."

Although Grandpa had lost his fight to save the lake, he didn't lose the fight to save the alligators. The county often issued permits for alligator hunters to capture animals that were in the way of human developments. The hunters were allowed to kill the alligators for their meat and skin. Grandpa wasn't against hunting any alligators, yet he was very much against his alligators being hunted. He had even held a fundraiser to pay for their relocation.

He noticed the frightened look on Lacey's face. "I'm not serious," said Grandpa. "I just hate to see all the changes that are going on."

The truck pulled up to the house. Three men got out. Grandpa hobbled off the porch to greet them. The men hardly paid attention to the alligators lurking at the edge of the yard.

"Cyrus LeBlanc?" said the driver as he extended his hand to Grandpa.

"The one and only," replied Grandpa.

“I figured you’d have these gators tied up and stacked waist deep by the time we got here,” the man said with a smile.

“I was just getting around to it,” smiled Grandpa. “Besides, I had to leave something for you to do.”

“It’s an honor to meet you,” said another man. “You’re a legend among gator wranglers.”

Grandpa smiled. One of the men looked toward the house and waved. Lacey waved back.

“It looks like you have your own gator wrangling crew,” said the man who waved.

Grandpa motioned for Lacey and Micah to come out of the house. They didn’t need to be asked twice. The screen door slapped against the house as it flung open. They were already off the porch before the spring pulled the door closed with a loud bang. The alligators at the edge stirred nervously at the sound.

“The big truck will be coming right along,” said the driver.

Grandpa looked at Lacey and Micah. “I want you on that porch when they start working those gators. If you can do that, you won’t have to be in the house. Do we have a deal?”

“Deal!” said Micah and Lacey together.

“They can even sit in the back of our truck if it’s all right with you. They’d be able to see everything,” suggested the driver to Grandpa.

Grandpa rubbed his chin in thought, “I guess this is probably the only time they’ll ever be able to see a gator round-up.” He looked sternly at Lacey and Micah. “But don’t take one step out of the truck unless I tell you.”

Micah and Lacey smiled brightly.

A loud rumble coming from the driveway announced the arrival of the bigger truck. A thin blond woman about the age of Micah and Lacey’s mother stepped out of the driver’s seat. She came over and gave Grandpa a big hug.

“It’s been a long time since I’ve seen you, Jessica,” smiled Grandpa.

“I think the last time was when you and Adel help us wrestle that twelve-foot alligator. He was a whopper,” said Jessica.

“What!” exclaimed Micah, “My mother wrestled an alligator?”

“All the time when she was younger,” said Grandpa. “Then she met your dad and decided it wasn’t quite lady-like.”

“What’s not lady-like about alligator wrestling?” smiled Jessica.

“It’s a mystery to me,” said Grandpa.

“Well, Boss now that you’re here we can get started,” said one of the men from the pick-up truck.

Jessica looked over the landscape. She walked closer to the alligators. There were four between her and the bank of the lake. One of them turned and looked at her. It was about twenty feet away. Jessica knelt down and looked at it at eye level.

"Hey fella, are you packed and ready to go to your new home?" she said softly.

One of the men walked up with a long pole. It had a loop of cable on the end.

"Should we start with that one?" asked the man.

"Yep, I think he's ready," said Jessica.

The children watched from the back of the pick-up truck. Their grandfather climbed up beside them.

"The first step is to snare the gator," explained Grandpa. "They slip the cable on the pole around the mouth of the gator. Then they'll draw it tight."

"Then what?" asked Lacey.

"Then the fun begins," said Grandpa. "They jump on his back and tape his mouth shut. Then they'll tape his back feet to keep him from crawling."

"Like handcuffs," said Lacey.

"Yep," said Grandpa. "They throw a towel over his eyes to calm him down. Then they'll carry him to the truck."

It happened just as Grandpa had described. Within a few hours, six alligators had been loaded. Grandpa was pretty sure that was all he had ever seen in the lake. He even recognized them and called them by name.

"Don't worry, Cyrus," said Jessica as she fastened the gate on the big truck. "We'll take good care of them."

"I know you will," said Grandpa.

He choked out the words. Lacey was sure she saw him wipe away a tear. Jessica gave Grandpa a hug.

"Tell Adel she can come wrestle gators with me anytime," smiled Jessica.

## Chapter 3
## Mystery in the Lake

"Can I ride in the wagon?" asked Lacey.

"Not while Micah is driving," said Grandpa.

"Will you teach me to drive the tractor next?" asked Lacey.

"Maybe when you turn thirteen," said Grandpa. "You have to be old enough to work the pedals."

"I know how," said Lacey. "That one is the clutch. That one is the brake. You move the lever on the steering wheel to speed up or slow down. You change gears with that metal bar."

"Very good!" said Grandpa. "Now all you have to do is wait for your legs to grow long enough to reach the clutch and brake."

Lacey backed away from the tractor. Grandpa told Micah to turn the key. The tractor started up. Lacey decided it was safest to watch from the porch of the house. Grandpa leaned on the fender of the tractor and stepped Micah through what to do next.

The tractor started off with a little bounce as Micah let out the clutch. Then the motor died.

"You let the clutch out a bit too quickly," said Grandpa. "Let's try it again and just ease off the clutch."

Micah mastered the take-off on the second try. He rode around the house. Lacey cheered after the first lap. The third time around the house, Grandpa instructed Micah to stop.

"Can I ride, now?" said Lacey.

"You've been patient," said Grandpa. "Micah, you're doing well, but I think I should be the one driving if Lacey is in the wagon."

"That's ok," said Micah. "It's fun to drive, but I like riding too."

Micah and Lacey hopped in the wagon. Grandpa sat on the tractor seat. When everyone was settled in, the tractor took off. They rode toward the lake.

They were all sad as they reached it. The housing development had started draining the lake a few days ago. The beautiful lake was replaced by a field of mud. The smell of rotting fish filled the air.

Grandpa stopped the tractor. He slid down from his seat. He walked toward the edge of the mud. Lacey and Micah joined him. Grandpa just shook his head sadly as he looked out over what was left of the lake.

“What’s that?” asked Lacey as she pointed to something several yards away from where they were standing.

“It looks like a pile of mud,” said Micah.

Grandpa squinted his eyes. He had a puzzled look on his face. He walked closer to the edge of the mud.

“I don’t have any idea what it is,” he said. “I’d sure like to find out. That mud looks pretty deep. Let’s go back to the barn and grab a few things.”

They rode back toward the house. Grandpa had a red barn that he pulled the tractor up next to.

“I’m going to need your help,” he said to Micah and Lacey. “I’ll need some planks to help me stay on top of the mud.”

Grandpa showed Micah and Lacey a neatly stacked pile of lumber. It looked old and weathered. Each board was about an inch thick, twelve inches wide, and six feet long. They each grabbed a board and carried it to the wagon. They made three more trips.

Next, Grandpa loaded up a heavy chain. Then he slipped off his shoes and put on a pair of rubber boots that came almost to his knees. He grabbed a few shovels and placed them next to the boards. Grandpa climbed back on the tractor. Micah and Lacey sat on the boards in the wagon. They returned to the lake.

As they approached the muddy land that was recently a lake, Lacey noticed something.

“Look Grandpa,” said Lacey. “It’s a path made of stones.”

Grandpa came over to her carrying a board. The path had been hidden by the water up until a few days ago. He studied the rocks. It wasn’t a natural pattern of rocks. Someone had built a path. It led toward the object in the lake.

He followed it down to the mud. Grandpa laid down the wooden plank. He stepped out on it. He expected it to sink several inches under his weight. Instead it sank a bit, but settled on something solid.

“Go get my cane from the tractor,” Grandpa instructed Micah.

Micah rushed to the tractor and ran back. “Here it is,” said Micah.

Grandpa took the cane and walked to the end of the first plank. He poked the cane into the mud directly in front of him. It only sank about an inch. He poked from left to right. Once he poked about three feet to his right, the cane sunk deeply in the mud. It did the same thing about four feet from his left. This matched the width of the path that had been under water. In fact, it was more like a bridge than a path.

With the mud so shallow over the stone path, Grandpa didn’t need the planks to get out to the object in the lake. He walked carefully. Grandpa kept poking the cane in the mud as he walked to trace the path. He was tired by the time he reached the object. It stuck out of the mud about two feet.

It was a plain round stone. Grandpa sat on it and rested. He ran his hands over the stone. It was about four inches thick and about eighteen inches in diameter. The top had something carved in it. Grandpa traced the grooves. It was some kind of a design.

“What is it?” asked Micah from the shore.

Grandpa stood up. He started walking back toward the bank of the lake. He followed his own muddy footsteps back in order to stay on the path. Micah helped him unhook the wagon from the tractor. Then Grandpa backed the tractor to the edge of the mud. The plan was to pull the stone to shore so it could be washed and read.

He hooked a chain to the tractor. Then Grandpa walked the chain out to the stone. He wrapped it around the stone. At the end of the chain was a hook. He hooked the chain to a link. Grandpa instructed Micah to get on the tractor. They were planning on pulling the stone to the shore.

Micah started the tractor. Following his grandfather's instructions, he put the tractor in its lowest gear. Micah slowly let out the clutch. The tractor rolled forward. The chain began to lift off the ground. It grew tight as the tractor began to pull the stone.

Grandpa was almost as tense as the chain. He wasn't sure this was the best thing to do. He didn't want the stone to break. He stepped closer as the stone began to move. If it began to show any sign of breaking, he would want to signal Micah to stop.

The grinding of stone against stone drew Grandpa closer. He was surprised to see the stone was setting on some kind of pedestal. The stone had moved about eight inches. Micah continued to pull with the tractor. Now, Grandpa's attention was drawn to the pedestal. He leaned over the stone.

Suddenly, a gush of water sprayed from the middle of the pedestal. The stone had moved enough to uncover a hole. The water shot straight into Grandpa's mouth. It soaked his shirt, then the rest of him.

Micah stopped. Grandpa quickly unhooked the chain. He went to the other side of the round stone. He was still being sprayed with the water. Grandpa leaned against the stone and was able to move it slightly. It was enough to stop the water. On shore Lacey giggled in delight. Her grandfather looked funny soaking wet.

## Chapter 4
## Grandpa's Surprise

Grandpa drove the tractor back to the house. He needed to get out of the wet clothes. Micah and Lacey rode in the wagon. The sun was beginning to set. Micah and Lacey were disappointed that they couldn't go back and explore the mystery in the lake.

Their grandfather hobbled off the tractor when they arrived at the house. He went up to his room, changed his clothes, and laid down. Micah and Lacey were used to him being tired in the evening, but tonight he fell right asleep. Micah was left fixing dinner for his sister and himself.

"I'm glad you like macaroni and cheese," said Micah.

"You're a good cook," said Lacey. "You should write a cookbook."

Micah scooped some macaroni into a bowl. "I'm going to check on Grandpa and see if he is hungry."

Micah walked up the stairs. He knocked softly on his grandfather's bedroom door. It was just loud enough to be heard if Grandpa was awake. It was soft enough not to wake him if he were asleep.

A voice did not answer. Instead there was a knocking sound from the other side of the door. Micah knocked again and listened for a response. Again, he heard a knocking sound. Micah slowly opened the door.

Grandpa's bed was empty. His window was open. Micah heard the sound again. This time it sounded more like a pounding sound. Micah walked to the window. Outside the window was the roof of a porch in the house.

Micah saw a strange sight. His grandfather was on the roof. He was replacing shingles. Grandpa positioned another shingle and pounded another nail. He stood on a ladder and worked quickly and energetically.

Grandpa looked up and saw Micah. His grandfather looked surprised.

“Micah! What are you doing here?” asked his grandfather.

“Bringing you some macaroni and cheese,” said Micah.

“You came all the way from Georgia to bring me some macaroni?”

“I came all the way from the kitchen,” said Micah. “We’ve been here for three days.”

“Three days?” Grandpa had a puzzled look on his face.

He climbed the ladder onto the roof. Grandpa scurried up the roof and climbed through the window. Micah stared in amazement. He’d never seen his grandfather move that quickly.

“You must really like macaroni!” said Micah.

“Thanks, Micah,” said Grandpa as he took the bowl. “Let’s go eat with everyone downstairs.”

Micah followed him to the kitchen. He noticed that his grandfather didn’t have any problem going down the steps. He didn’t hobble or limp in the least. Grandpa walked into the kitchen.

“Well, hi Lacey!” said Grandpa happily. “My, you’ve grown so much!”

“Since this afternoon?” asked Lacey.

“Where’s your mom and dad?” asked Grandpa.

“In the Bahamas,” said Lacey. “Don’t you remember?”

Grandpa opened the refrigerator. He pulled out a package of hamburger. Lacey watched her grandfather. He not only acted differently, he looked different. His hair was a less gray. He seemed thinner.

“I think that water washed some of the gray out of your hair,” said Lacey.

Grandpa smiled as he made hamburger patties. Micah looked closely at the hair. It did seem different. Micah remembered the pictures of his grandfather holding Lacey as a baby. His grandfather looked about the same age as he did in Lacey’s baby pictures.

“Looks like I’m cooking the burgers,” said Grandpa. “I’ll put them out on the grill.”

He formed patties and placed them on a plate. He grabbed some spices from a cabinet and sprinkled it on the meat. Grandpa worked happily. He even hummed softly.

“I wonder when your grandma will be back?” asked Grandpa. “Do you know where she went?”

Now, Micah was getting worried. His grandmother had died three years ago. His grandfather had never looked healthier, but Micah was beginning to think he was sick. Maybe the water from the lake was causing some problem with Grandpa’s memory.

Lacey looked at her grandfather strangely. “I think grandma went to heaven.”

Suddenly, Grandpa stopped working. He stopped smiling. Grandpa pulled out a chair and sat down. His eyebrows wrinkled as he strained to think.

“That’s right,” he said softly and sadly. “It’s been years ago. I…I don’t know what I was thinking.”

Lacey leaned her head on his shoulder, “It’s okay grandpa. You still have us!”

Grandpa smiled and gave Lacey a hug, “That I do! I have two fine grandchildren here with me that need to be fed. Now let’s get these burgers on the grill.”

Grandpa lit some charcoal in an old barbecue grill. Lacey enjoyed watching the flames from the lighter fluid dance. She also liked the smoky smell. Grandpa warned Lacey not to touch it, and then went back into the house.

He came out a minute later. Micah expected him to be carrying the plate of hamburgers. Instead, he carried three baseball gloves and a baseball.

“I thought we could play a little catch while the charcoals get good and hot,” said Grandpa.

The three of them tossed the ball around. Lacey thought it was great fun. She had never seen her grandfather be so active. He chased balls and even fielded the grounders she threw him.

## Chapter 5
## Ponce de Leon

The sound of the tractor got Micah out of bed early the next morning. The sun had not been up for more than a half-hour. He had heard his grandfather stirring about his room. Then he heard him walk down the steps. It was a more familiar sound. Grandpa moved much more slowly than he did the previous day.

Micah was curious about his grandfather. He dressed quickly and ran out the door. He could see the tractor in the distance. Grandpa was heading to the lake.

He followed at a distance. The sound of the tractor had slowed. Micah thought about joining his grandfather, but decided to hide behind a cypress tree and watch. In some ways it was a repeat of the day before.

Grandpa hooked the chain around the stone. He got on the tractor and slowly pulled until the fountain sprung into the air. Grandpa this time deliberately got wet. He drank in as much water as he could. Then he pushed the stone back into place. The water stopped.

Micah watched as his grandfather drove the tractor past the cypress tree. His grandfather had already parked the tractor and gone to his room by the time Micah reached the house. He went to his own room. Micah put his ear up against the wall to listen into the next room.

His grandfather opened drawers and then the closet door. He was obviously changing out of the wet clothes. Next, Micah heard the squeaking of the old box springs of Grandpa's bed. Finally, a familiar snoring sound could be heard. Micah didn't need to put his ear to the wall to hear that. Grandpa was sound asleep.

A few hours later he was still not awake. Micah was again fixing a meal. This time it was toast and jelly. Lacey had two pieces.

"You are a really good cook," said Lacey. "Maybe you should open a restaurant."

"Macaroni and toast, I think, as a chef, I would starve," smiled Micah.

"It would be sad if the person who made the food starved," said Lacey.

A door opened upstairs. Lacey and Micah stopped talking as they heard footsteps. They were moving quickly.

"Good morning!" said Grandpa as he stepped into the kitchen.

Lacey looked confused. The man in the kitchen didn't look like her grandfather. He looked a lot like her uncle Alex. That was her mother's older brother.

"What's wrong Adel? Why are you looking at me so strangely?" asked Grandfather. She just stared in bewilderment.

He looked over at Micah. "What's up with her, Xander?" That's what their grandfather called their uncle Alexander.

Now Lacey was really confused. The man standing in the kitchen looked like her Uncle Alexander. Yet it couldn't be. He thought Micah was Alexander. She just hoped her Uncle Alexander didn't make a surprise visit. Then everyone would be totally confused.

Micah looked at his grandfather. He was beginning to understand what was happening.

"We're not your kids," explained Micah. "We're your grandchildren. Adel is our mother."

Grandpa sat down at the table. He looked into the faces of Lacey and Micah. He thought hard, forcing himself to remember.

"Yes," said Grandpa. "It's coming back to me. And your grandmother…"

"Three years ago," Micah added softly.

Grandpa rested his face in his hands. His mind raced with memories from the past. He felt the happy times and the sad times all over again. After a few minutes, he raised his head.

He looked at his hands. They were a lot less wrinkled than they were the day before. He flexed his fingers. The joints were painless when his fingers moved. Then he noticed a scar that was ten years old was completely gone.

"What's happening to me?" asked Grandpa. "My body feels so strong and well. Still, my mind is so confused."

"I think it's the fountain," said Micah. "Every time you drink it, or get soaked in the water, you change."

"Change? How do I change?" asked Grandpa.

"You get younger and you have trouble remembering the past," said Micah.

"Yesterday, you played baseball with us," added Lacey.

"And this all happened after I drank from the fountain?" asked Grandpa.

"Yes," said Micah.

Grandpa rose from the table and walked out of the room. Micah and Lacey followed him. They walked into the living room. There were bookshelves on each side of the television. Grandpa scanned the titles. He pulled a large book off the shelf.

He sat in a chair and thumbed through it. Micah and Lacey looked over his shoulders. Grandpa found what he was looking for and started reading silently.

"This is it!" he said excitedly.

Lacey read the caption under a picture, "Ponce de Leon?"

"I remember studying about him," said Micah. "He explored Florida."

"That's right," said Grandpa. "Some people believe he was looking for a fountain of youth. There were stories from the native tribes about a fountain that kept people from aging."

"And they found it in your lake?" asked Lacey. "Read to me the part that talks about your lake."

"It doesn't talk about my lake," said Grandpa. "They never found the fountain. Well, at least that's what the history books say. Some aren't even sure Ponce was looking for the fountain."

"Wait until everyone finds out," said Lacey. "They'll be bazillions of people coming to drink from it."

Suddenly Grandpa looked wide-eyed. "I don't want bazillions of people coming here. We'd never get any peace. They'd trample everything. Can you imagine the mess huge crowds of people would make of this place?"

Grandpa convinced Micah and Lacey that the world wasn't ready to discover the fountain of youth. They agreed to tell no one about their great find. Grandpa said he was tired of the history lesson. He wanted to do something different today. He went out to the barn and found three old bicycles that had been stored for years.

They washed them off. Grandpa pumped up the tires with an old hand pump. He oiled the chains and tightened some bolts. They spent the rest of the day on a bike ride through the countryside.

# Chapter 6
## Like a Brother

The next few days followed the same pattern. Grandpa would wake up with the sunrise. He would be his old self with achy joints and wrinkled skin. He would hop onto the tractor and go to the fountain.

He would return to the house soaking wet. Grandpa would change clothes and go back to sleep for a few hours. Each day he came down the steps after Micah and Lacey were awake. He grew younger each day he drank from the fountain.

Each day, Micah would once again tell Grandpa who he was. He struggled more and more to remember the past. Micah was patient with his grandfather and had even started using a family picture album to remind him of family members.

That gave Lacey an idea. She suggested they take pictures of themselves with their grandfather to help him remember. That way he could see that he was getting younger every day, and that they weren't.

This morning was the most unusual yet. First of all, Micah couldn't even make toast because they were out of bread. In fact, they were running out of all kinds of grocery supplies. The last few days Grandpa had become less serious and more playful. He didn't want to do boring things such as shopping.

When Grandpa came down the stairs this morning, he actually slid down on the rail. Then he mistook Lacey and Micah for his cousins Myra and Luke. The most amazing part was that grandpa didn't look much older than Micah. In fact, he was wearing Micah's clothes.

He didn't ask about their grandmother, their mother, or Uncle Alexander. He didn't remember ever being married. He didn't remember having children. Yet, after Micah explained things to him and Lacey showed him their picture collection, he began to remember.

After finding out they had nothing to eat, Grandpa zipped up the stairs. He came back down with the car keys in one hand and his wallet in the other.

"Let's hop in the car and take a trip to the grocery store. I can't wait to drive. It sounds really fun!" said Grandpa.

Lacey and Micah got into the back seat of the car. Grandpa sat in the driver's seat. He had to adjust it forward. He was shorter today because he was younger than he was when he hit his growth spurt. He needed to reach the pedals.

When they got to the grocery store, they began walking up and down the aisles. Grandpa only wanted to buy cookies, soft drinks, and snack cakes. Micah had to talk him into buying some "real food" too.

Lacey went down an aisle. Micah followed with the cart.

"What are you looking for here?" asked Micah.

"We should probably get some baby food and diapers," replied Lacey.

"Why?" asked Micah as he kept an eye on his grandfather out the corner of his eye. Grandpa had found a rack of candy.

"Only one bag," Micah told his grandpa.

Grandpa frowned and kept shopping.

"Look at Grandpa," said Lacey as she pointed toward the candy. "He gets younger every day. He may be a baby by tomorrow."

Micah had to agree. He picked out a baby bottle and pacifier just in case. They wheeled their cart to the check-out. Grandpa saw the total on the cash register. He thumbed through his wallet.

He didn't have enough cash. Grandpa pulled out a credit card and swiped it though the machine. He punched in another number. The cashier completed the sale and handed Grandpa the receipt.

They wheeled the cart with sacks of groceries out the door and into the parking lot. They didn't notice the cashier talking to the customer behind them in the line and pointing. It was a sheriff's deputy. She was questioning why a young teenager would have a credit card.

It seemed strange to her. The deputy agreed. He decided to check things out. After leaving the store he looked around the parking lot. He noticed the three loading groceries into the trunk of the car.

By the time he reached them, Grandpa was in the driver's seat. Micah and Lacey were putting on their seat belts in the back seat. The deputy tapped on the window. Grandpa and Lacey both lowered their windows.

The deputy leaned over and looked Grandpa in the eye. "Aren't you a little young to be driving?"

"No," answered Grandpa. "I've been driving for years, young man."

“Sure,” said the deputy. “Then may I see your license?”

Grandpa opened his wallet and pulled it out. The deputy looked it over. He studied the picture, and then looked back at Grandpa.

“From the looks of this you’ve been driving for about sixty years before you were born. That’s a pretty neat trick. You’ll need to step out of the car,” said the deputy.

Just then, a man walked up. Lacey recognized him from the grocery store. A few times it seemed like he was following them around.

“Is there a problem, deputy?” asked the stranger as he handed a small bag of groceries to Lacey through the window.

“Is it any business of yours?” asked the officer.

“Has my nephew done anything wrong?” asked the stranger.

“He was getting ready to drive,” said the officer.

“And leave me behind?” said the man. “Why would they do that?”

The officer looked confused. “He was sitting in the driver’s seat.”

“He’s about to turn fifteen,” explained the stranger. “He likes to sit there when we’re parked and review where everything is. I’m sorry if that caused any confusion. If there’s a law against it, I’ll make sure his parents know not to let him do it again.”

The deputy thought for a moment. “I can’t think of a law against it.”

“Well, we bought some ice cream for his grandfather,” said the man, “along with the other groceries. May we go on before things melt?”

The officer sighed, “I guess so. I’m sorry to detain you.”

“No problem, Deputy,” said the man as he motioned for Grandpa to slide over to the passenger side of the car seat.

The stranger got in the driver’s seat as the deputy watched. There was nothing to do except to start the engine and drive away.

As soon as they were at the edge of the parking lot, the man asked, “Where am I driving you?”

“To the next parking lot and then get out,” said Grandpa.

The man glanced in the rearview mirror. “I don’t think that’s a good idea.”

Grandpa looked in the mirror too. The deputy’s car was right behind them.

“Turn left,” sighed Grandpa.

The deputy also turned left. Grandpa kept giving directions to the way home. The deputy continued to follow them. They didn’t know if it was because the deputy was suspicious or just happened to be traveling the same direction.

Grandpa lived off the main highway just outside of town, so it was possible the deputy wasn’t trying to follow them. Grandpa didn’t want to risk any more questions from the officer. He decided to let the man drive them all the way home.

## Chapter 7
## Stranger and Stranger

"My name is Roger Picard," said the man as he drove. "I apologize for forcing my way into your situation like I did. I just didn't see things getting any easier for anyone if the deputy kept asking questions."

"What situation?" asked Grandpa. He didn't want to admit anything to the stranger, especially the fact that he was years older than he looked.

"I saw you drive up," said Roger. "I was walking across the parking lot from the bus station. I just got into town and wanted to buy some food. I hope your parents won't mind if we go back to the station later and get my luggage."

Grandpa wasn't sure about the stranger. The man told the deputy a lie, even though it did help them out. Grandpa had hoped they could drop the man off somewhere in town. He didn't want anyone to learn about his secret, let alone someone he didn't know or trust.

"I'm sure your parents will be worried," said the man as he drove down the gravel driveway to Grandpa's house.

"Our parents are in the Bahamas," said Lacey as they arrived at the house. "This is Grandpa's house."

The car pulled up to the house. Everyone got out. Micah and Lacey helped their grandfather unload the groceries. Even the stranger helped.

"Maybe your grandfather can drive me back into town," said the man as he looked around the kitchen.

"I think he might be napping," said Grandpa. "I'll go check on him."

Grandpa went up the stairs. He came back a minute later.

"Grandpa isn't here," said Grandpa. "I'm not sure when he'll get back. I'm sure he wouldn't want a stranger here alone with us kids."

"Maybe you're right," said the stranger. "Or maybe you don't want your grandfather to know you took his car. I'm really going to need to talk to him."

"Okay," said Grandpa. "Now that we have groceries put away, maybe we should go get your luggage at the bus station."

The four of them drove back to town. Roger parked at the bus station. As soon as he went inside, Grandpa slid over in the seat.

"Roger took the keys," said Micah.

"I know," said Grandpa as he reached into his pocket. "I have another key. I got it from my room when we went home."

He started to put the key into the ignition. Just then a deputy's car pulled up next to them. Grandpa slid back over the passenger's side. The door to the bus station opened. Roger smiled and waved at us. He walked to the back of the car and opened the trunk. He placed two bags in the back. Roger got back into the car.

"I'm surprised you didn't take off without me," he smiled. "Do you suppose your grandfather is home yet?"

"He's not home," said Lacey.

"She means, we don't think he's home yet," added Micah.

"He may be there when we get back," said Roger. "You seem like nice kids. Why would you take your grandfather's car?"

"To get groceries," answered Lacey.

Grandpa began laughing at the answer.

"Driving when you're too young is very serious," scolded Roger. "This car is not a toy. It's a responsibility. I hope your grandfather is ready to take action."

When they arrived at the house, Roger took his luggage from the trunk. He carried it to the front porch and sat down. The other three went into the house. Lacey came back carrying a bag.

"Here are your groceries. I thought you might be hungry," she said.

“Thanks,” said Roger. “That was very thoughtful of you.”

Micah peeked out the window. Grandpa had told him to keep an eye on him.

“Is he still there?” asked Grandpa.

“Yes, he’s sitting on a chair. He’s eating a sandwich and talking to Lacey,” Micah fed him the details.

“Do you think he’ll give up and leave?” asked Grandpa.

“I don’t think so,” said Micah. “He looks pretty comfortable. I think he’s prepared to spend the night right there on the porch if he has to.”

“I suppose if I had caught some young child driving a car, I would insist on talking to his parents too,” said Grandpa. “Still, I can’t get over the feeling he wants something else. It’s just very strange, the way he just hopped in the car and started driving.”

“Do you think he’s dangerous,” asked Micah. “Should I go get Lacey?”

“I’ll go out there,” said Grandpa. “I don’t think he’s dangerous, but you never know. Stay in here. If he tries anything, call the police.”

Grandpa went out to the porch. “My grandfather left a note. He wrote that it would be late before he came back. I can drive you to the end of the driveway. You could catch a ride back in town. You can still talk to my grandfather about the driving, tomorrow.”

Roger reached into the bag. He pulled out a bottle of chocolate milk. He opened it up and took a drink. A look of satisfaction spread on his face.

“This is really good stuff. I wish they had it when I was growing up,” said Roger.

“Chocolate milk?” asked Lacey. “They didn’t have that when you were growing up?”

“No,” smiled Roger. “We would have to heat up chocolate and milk on an old wood burning stove. You couldn’t walk into stores and buy a bottle of chocolate milk in the 1860’s.”

“Are you saying you grew up in the 1860’s?” asked Grandpa.

“I was born in 1857, in Virginia. Is that so hard to believe, Grandpa?” Roger asked.

Lacey was surprised that Roger called her grandfather, Grandpa.

“I’ve known all along,” said Roger. “In fact, I came to find this place.”

“How did you know I was older than I looked?” asked Grandpa.

“Well, first you were driving. Then all the clothes you are wearing would fit your grandson better than they fit you. Plus, your grandkids called you Grandpa in the grocery store.”

## Chapter 8
## Roger's Story

That night, Roger told quite a story.

"I was always intrigued by the legends about the fountain of youth," said Roger. "A mysterious map had been given to me by my father. The story was that it came from one of our ancestors that lived about the time Florida was explored by Ponce de Leon. The map was made by a chief of the Seminole tribe. The Seminoles were the people who lived in this area before the Europeans came."

"This ancestor had been shipwrecked and washed onto a Florida beach. He became friends with the Seminoles and eventually married one of the chief's daughters. Before he could find the fountain, more explorers came back. He returned with them and his wife to Puerto Rico."

"I had tossed the map in a trunk and there is stayed for years. As I grew older, I began to think about the map again. It was the summer of 1921. I had just turned 64 years old."

"I told my family I was heading to New York on business. Instead I came to Florida to search for the fountain. After searching a few days, I came upon some bubbling water that I thought was a spring. It was a hot day and I was very thirsty. The water was cool and sweet."

"I walked back to the mule drawn wagon where I made my camp. I feel asleep in the back of the wagon. Several hours later, I woke up. Something strange had happened to me. I felt younger than I had in years."

"Day after day I was drawn back to the fountain. Each time I grew younger and younger. I'm surprised I didn't end up as a baby. On the twelfth day, I stopped getting younger. In fact, I ended up just as I am now."

"I no longer craved the water from the fountain. I returned home to Virginia, not realizing how much I had changed. I returned home because of the childhood memories, but I didn't remember my wife or son. I was in town a few days before I saw my wife again. Then I started to remember. The problem was my wife and son did not recognize me. I appeared younger than my own son."

"I tried to convince them by telling details about our lives, things that only we would know. This only convinced them that I was someone who did some evil to me. They thought I was someone who met up with me and told stories."

"My grandson, who was 14 at the time, was the only one who would listen to my story about the fountain of youth. When the old me didn't return home after several weeks, my son planned to have me arrested. My grandson warned me."

"I got so desperate, I kidnapped my wife. I brought her to the fountain. I thought if we could both drink of the fountain, we could both not grow old together. It didn't have the same effect on her. She never changed."

"By this time, not only did she not believe it was me; she thought I was some madman. She escaped and wandered about the swamp," tears formed as he continued the story. "I found her after two days. She didn't survive the swamp."

"My son and his family moved to California, and I never spoke to him again. I felt so awful. Even if he had believed my story, he probably still would have hated me. So I didn't try to find him. I had given up all hope of finding any family again until a few weeks ago. There are websites where you can find out about your ancestors."

"I was doing research on one, not to find ancestors, but to find my descendents. I had checked for years, but none of my grandson's descendents had searched our family records. Then one day, it was there. Someone had filled out the information for my grandson's children, grandchildren, and even great grandchildren."

"It was my great, great, great granddaughter Shelby. I sent her a message saying I was asking about her great, grandfather. She told me where to find my grandson's grave. He must have kept trying to help me, for there on his tombstone was a message for me. It simply said: To Roger, the Riddle on the Bridge."

"I asked Shelby if she knew what it meant. She said that her great grandfather told her mom a strange story about his grandfather drinking from the fountain of youth. He spent most of his life looking for his grandfather and any clues he could get to help him. She said that was the only clue he ever found, and he didn't even know what it meant."

"That's when I decided to come back here. If I can find the riddle of the bridge, maybe it will help me start to age again."

"Why do you want to grow old?" asked Lacey.

"Everyone I've loved has grown old and died. I found that wherever I live, I can only stay until people start wondering why I haven't aged. Then I have to move and start all over. My body hasn't aged, but my mind has. It's become like a bad dream that I can't wake up from."

"I don't know what riddle of the bridge means," said Grandpa,

"But Grandpa," said Micah, "We do know where there is a bridge."

"You're right, Micah," said Grandpa. "We may not have a riddle, but we have a bridge. We'll do some investigating first thing in the morning."

## Chapter 9
## Riddle of the Bridge

The next morning, Grandpa woke up early. This time he didn't ride the tractor to the fountain. Instead he gathered up shovels, brooms, and buckets. He filled the buckets with water.

He worked slower this morning because he had his old body once again. Micah looked out the window and saw his grandfather working. Micah dressed quickly and ran down the stairs.

Grandpa asked Micah to get the tractor and hook up the wagon. Micah noticed something different about his grandfather. He looked like he did before discovering the fountain, yet he acted differently. Grandpa seemed happier, more peaceful.

"Are Lacey and Roger awake yet?" asked Grandpa.

Just then, Lacey came out of the house. She carried a plate.

"I cooked breakfast," said Lacey. "It's a special recipe, toast and jelly."

Grandpa took a bite, "Very tasty. Maybe you should write a cookbook."

Lacey smiled, "Actually, it's Micah's recipe."

"Did you fix Roger some toast?" asked Micah.

"No," said Lacey. "He wasn't in the house."

"I think I know where he is," said Grandpa as he sat down on the wagon. "Micah, drive us to the fountain."

They rode back to the fountain. Sure enough, Roger was sitting on the round stone waiting for them. The mud around the fountain had begun to dry. Grandpa directed Roger and Micah to dump the buckets of water on the bridge.

They scooped the mud and dirt from the rocks. Lacey was the first one to discover a letter. It was the letter n. She uncovered more letters until she could read the word "again." It was carved into one of the stones that made the bridge.

This got everyone excited. They worked throughout the day. Micah brought buckets of water from the house. Letter by letter, they uncovered words on the bridge. Roger was hopeful he would soon be able to read the riddle of the bridge. By lunchtime they stood back and looked at their work.

"What does it mean?" asked Micah as they read the words.

*Do not drink for ten and twain*
*For at mid-life's age you will remain*
*Till for all those loved you feel sorrow's pain*
*And drink from the fountain once again.*

"Ten and twain is ten plus two," said Roger. "I drank from the fountain twelve times. That's what made the change permanent."

"And you remained this same age for all these years," said Micah.

"Til for all those loved you feel sorrow's pain," said Grandpa sadly as he thought of his wife. "I can't imagine how it would feel to lose everyone you ever cared about. I think you've felt sorrow for all you lost."

"And drink from the fountain once again," read Lacey. "Is that why your wife didn't change? Was it because you had to feel the pain of losing her?"

Roger sighed, "You might be right."

Grandpa pointed to the round stone that blocked the water, "Do you think you could move that stone?"

"I think so," said Roger.

"That's your solution," said Grandpa as he patted Roger on the shoulder. "Drink from the fountain once again."

Grandpa picked up a shovel and walked back to the wagon. Micah and Lacey picked up tools and followed. They left the fountain with Roger sitting on the round stone. The rumble of the tractor echoed around the woods as Micah drove it back to the house.

Roger looked around him. It brought back memories over a century old. He thought of all he had seen in his lifetime. He had seen wars and lived in times of peace. He had seen people born and then die at a ripe old age. He lived at a time when people traveled by slow wagons and super sonic jets.

Everything about him had changed. He had remained the same. He remembered being afraid of growing old before he found the fountain. After that, he feared never growing old. Roger decided it was time to change. He stood up and rolled back the stone.

Grandpa, Micah, and Lacey could tell he was different as he came up to the house. There was just a touch of gray in his hair. His walk was a bit slower. There were a few more creases in his forehead.

Roger had aged, just a bit. He didn't turn old all at once. There was just enough of a change to be a promise. There was more to come, more wrinkles, more gray hairs, more little aches and pains.

They drove him to the bus station that day. On the trip back, Lacey asked her grandfather what would happen to Roger now. Grandpa gave an answer that was different than he might have given a few days before.

"He'll start living again," said Grandpa. "He can fit in with everyone else now. Maybe he'll even meet some nice lady and get married."

"It reminds me of something I learned at church," said Micah. "Whoever seeks to keep his life will lose it, and whoever loses his life will preserve it."

"It's something like that," Grandpa nodded in agreement.

## Chapter 10
## A Bucket of Gators

Grandpa directed the dump truck down the path. Someone at some other time had hidden the fountain in a lake. The water was gone, so now it would have to be covered with dirt. The people from the construction site were grateful to have such a close place to dump the extra dirt they didn't need.

Lacey and Micah stood with Grandpa. They watched as the fountain was hidden from view. After awhile Lacey grew tired of watching the mound of dirt grow. Something in the tall grass by the old edge of the lake caught her eye.

"Do you have chickens?" Lacey asked her grandfather.

"No," said Grandpa.

"Then why do you have so many eggs?" she asked.

Grandpa came over to her. He bent over and looked in the grass. Several eggs were tucked out of sight. Grandpa walked back to the wagon and grabbed a bucket. He carefully moved the eggs.

Grandpa pointed to a hole in one of the eggs. Lacey watched carefully. The egg shook slightly. The hole grew a little larger. After awhile she could see a little nose peeking through.

"It's an alligator!" said Lacey. "It's so cute."

"Will they all hatch?" asked Micah.

"Probably not," answered Grandpa. "But a few of them might."

Grandpa was right. By the time their parents arrived that afternoon, three alligators scurried about the bucket.

"I hope they didn't wear you out," said Adel to her dad as she spoke about Lacey and Micah.

"I haven't felt younger in years," smiled Grandpa. "In fact, I almost felt younger than them."

Lacey and Micah both laughed at the comment.

"Hey Mom, do you want to wrestle the alligators?" teased Micah.

"What have you been telling them?" Adel said to her father.

"Just the truth about their old alligator wrangling mom," smiled Grandpa.

"I never knew that!" said Micah and Lacey's dad. "Wait until all our friends back home hear about this!"

"If you tell them, Joseph, I'll wrangle you!" warned Adel. "That goes double for you, two." She turned Lacey and Micah.

"What are you going to do with the alligators?" asked Lacey.

"They can't stay here," said Grandpa. "I made a phone call this afternoon to a friend of mine. There's a zoo in Atlanta that will take them. Only thing is their budget is kind of tight. They need someone to volunteer to help raise them for a few months."

"Does this mean you are coming home with us?" smiled Adel.

"If your offer is still open, I'd like to give it a try," said Grandpa.

"We'd love to have more time with you," said Joe.

"Yes," said Adel as she hugged her dad. "Sometimes I wish you could just turn time back and do things all over again. Don't you dad?"

"Not any more," said Grandpa. "Not any more."

"I would rather Grandpa be my grandpa. Not my little brother," said Lacey.

"Where do you get such funny ideas?" smiled her mom.

# Forms of Poetry

A **syllable cinquain** has a pattern of syllables. The first line has two syllables and is the title. The second line has 4 syllables and describes the title. The third line has 6 syllables that describes some action. Line four has 8 syllables and describes a feeling. Line five is a synonym of the title or another description and has 2 syllables.

## Syllable Cinquain

**Popcorn**
Buttered, crunchy
Eating at the movies
Happy we could share a big tub
Great treat!

## Word Cinquain

**Ice**
Cold, hard
Cooling my drink
So refreshing in lemonade
Cubes

In a **word cinquain**, the first line is a single word title and topic. The next line is 2 words that are adjectives for the title. Line three is a 3 word phrase that provides more information. Line four is 4 words that describe a feeling. Line five is a 1 word synonym or reference to the title.

A **haiku** is a three line poem about nature. It has three lines. The first line is 5 syllables. The second line has 7 syllables. The third line had 5 syllables.

## Haiku

**Puppies in a box**
Rumbling, Tumbling balls of fur
Barking, yelping, fun

A **limerick** is a five line poem that follows a rhyming and accent pattern. Lines 1, 2, and 5 rhyme. They each have three stressed syllables. Lines 3 and 4 rhyme and have two stressed syllables.

## Limerick

***My First Race***

I wanted to win my first race
For awhile I kept up with the pace
But my shoe came untied
And I certainly cried
When I tripped and fell on my face

Made in the USA
Monee, IL
13 June 2023